GETTING A JOB AFTER COLLEGE

JOB SEARCH STRATEGIES AND INTERVIEW PREPARATION THAT WILL GET YOU HIRED

ROBERT MOMENT

GETTING A JOB AFTER COLLEGE

JOB SEARCH STRATEGIES AND INTERVIEW PREPARATION THAT WILL GET
YOU HIRED

© 2018 ROBERT MOMENT

ISBN-978-0-9864493-2-1

Visit www.GettingaJobAfterCollege.com to learn more about Job Search Strategies and Interview Preparation That Will Get Hired.

GETTING A JOB AFTER COLLEGE

JOB SEARCH STRATEGIES AND INTERVIEW PREPARATION
THAT WILL GET YOU HIRED

Contents

Introduction vi

CHAPTER 1

Believe In Yourself For Career Success 1

How to Achieve Success 1

The Keys to Success 3

CHAPTER 2

15 Ways To Stay Motivated During Your Job Search 7

Set Up a Job Search Schedule (Daily, Weekly, Monthly) 12

CHAPTER 3

How To Write A Cover Letter That Stands Out And Lands Job Interviews 17

Writing a Cover Letter Introduction 26

The Secret to Writing the Perfect Cover Letter Introduction 28

5 Step surefire formula on how to write a cover letter
that will land a job interview 30

Top ten cover letter writing mistakes to avoid 31

CHAPTER 4

25 Resume Writing Tips That Will Get You Hired 35

Top Ten Resume Writing Mistakes to Avoid 42

CHAPTER 5

25 Job Search Strategies Every College Graduate Should Know 47

CHAPTER 6

25 Job Interview Preparation That Will Help You Land A Job 57

CHAPTER 7

15 Interview Skills That Will Get You Hired 63

CHAPTER 8

**90 Interview Questions And The Best Answers You
Need To Know For Successful Job Interviews** 69

CHAPTER 9

10 Keys To A Successful Telephone Job Interview 105

CHAPTER 10

**10 Things Interviewers And Hiring Managers Look
For In Job Candidates (Top Soft Skills)** 109

Examples of Soft Skill Questions 114
Ways to Build Soft Skills 115

CHAPTER 11

**10 Ways To Leave A Lasting Impression With
Interviewers And Hiring Managers** 117

CHAPTER 12

**How To Turn A Job Interview Into A Job Offer - 7
Steps To Make A Connection And Get Hired** 123

Step One: Understanding the Difference between Assets and Value. 124
Step Two: Understanding Business Pain 126
Step Three: Finding Business Pain with Probing Questions 126
Step Four: Selling Your Problem Solving Skills 127
Step Five: Building Emotional Trust as the "Must Hire." 128
Step Six: Asking For the Job 129
Step Seven: Sending a Thank You Letter 130
25 Brilliant Questions to Ask Interviewers or Hiring Managers 131

CHAPTER 13

How To Follow Up After A Job Interview 139

Tips for Writing a Strong Thank You Email.................................. 143

Reference.. 143

CHAPTER 14

How To Negotiate A Salary–Get What You Deserve 145

CHAPTER 15

Dress For Success–Image Is Everything! 153

The Formal Interview 153

Women 154

Men 154

Business Casual 155

Six things you should never wear to an interview.......................... 156

CHAPTER 16

How To Create An Effective 30-60-90 Day Employment Action Plan (Hiring Managers Will Love This) 159

How to Create a Successful 30-60-90 Day
Employment Action Plan That Will Impress Hiring
Managers and Secure Employment.. 159

How to Write a 30-60-90 Day Action Plan 162

The Bottom Line... 168

Conclusion 171

About The Author 175

Introduction

Congratulations on Your Graduation!

Dear Recent Graduate:

You made it! You've earned your degree, and now it's time to take what you've learned out into the real world to begin your career. Whatever field you've chosen, you'll need to get your foot in the door in order to secure a position and then advance accordingly. If the prospect seems intimidating or you're not sure where to start, just remember that you're not alone. This book will help!

Master What Most College Courses Don't Prepare You For

Getting a Job After College: Job Search Strategies and Interview Preparation That Will Get You Hired was written to bridge that often-scary gap between college grad and employed adult. Years of courses in your chosen discipline taught you plenty about making it in that industry, but they probably didn't cover the basics of getting hired.

That's where this ultimate guide for getting hired out of col-lege comes in. We've researched today's job market, where companies look for qualified candidates and how they choose who gets interviewed. *Getting a Job After College: Job Search Strategies and Interview Preparation That Will Get You Hired* covers all of this plus the very best strategies for nailing the interview process. Read it cover to cover and/or skip to specific sections as you need them. Inside you'll learn in detail how to:

- Conduct an efficient job search that gets results
- How to best present yourself even if you have little to no work experience
- Write a killer cover letter that cannot be ignored
- Create a resume that gets you noticed and selected for interviews
- Ace an interview and win the offer
- Tackle the 90 most common interview questions
- Negotiate your salary
- Earn attractive offers from companies you're interested in
- And more

It's a tough market out there. Even the best students are up against intense competition when it comes to finding the perfect job—or any job—after college. *Getting a Job After College: Job Search Strategies and Interview Preparation That Will Get You Hired* teaches you what college simply doesn't prepare you for and provides the tools you need to find your first real job!

If you don't know where to begin or lack critical job search skills, this book is for you! If you are close to graduating or already finding it hard to get a job, read the book!   If you know you should brush up on your interview skills, get the book. Job hunting success need not elude you. You can do this and Getting a Job After College: Job Search Strategies and Interview Preparation That Will Get You Hired will help you get there.

Your successful career awaits! Start reading this book and stand out from the competition. The sooner you do it, the sooner you'll land that amazing job you've always wanted.

Get hired by the companies you want to work for TODAY!

Believe In Yourself For Career Success

Success is something that all of us desire in life, whether it is to become rich, reach the top of the corporate ladder or simply to take care of family. Achieving success takes more than just the will to do it, you need a plan, education and the right approach.

You cannot start on the road to success unless you believe in yourself first. If you don't believe success will happen, you will miss it. The key to success starts with learning to believe in yourself and thereby gaining the confidence you need to get the results you desire.

How to Achieve Success

It all begins with believing in yourself, which is actually a little harder to do than you may realize. It's not just telling yourself that you can do it. You have to build your confidence, experience and knowledge in order to become successful. In addition, your belief in yourself will grow as you accomplish each task.

Define it

Success is whatever you determine it to be. You must first examine your definition of success. Define your goals. Have a clear picture of what you want to achieve and do not let others decide for you.

Set Goals

You cannot succeed in life if you don't have a roadmap to success, just as you cannot get anywhere if you don't know where you are going. While many of us are familiar with the general idea of what we want to accomplish, we don't set the necessary goals to attain success.

Write down your goals. Start with your long term goal of achieving what you want and then have a series of short term goals that will get you to your ultimate prize. Think of it as a ladder with each step being a short term goal with your ultimate achievement resting at the top.

Embrace Failure

It may sound strange, but part of becoming successful is failing on your first, second, fifth, tenth or twentieth attempt. Failure has been a part of every successful invention that has had any meaningful impact in history.

Consider Thomas Edison, who invented the incandescent light bulb over a century ago. He failed over 10,000 times before he finally got the right combination of materials to create the bulb that would dominate the 20th century. Yet Edison not only kept pressing on after failing, he actually embraced his failures and called them learning ways that did not work toward his ultimate goal.

Could you imagine failing 100 times and not stopping? Edison failed over 10,000 times and today is a legend because of his achievements. You have the same capacity as Edison in learning from and embracing failure as part of your long term success.

Sacrifice

Unfortunately, to achieve your desire it will require sacrificing something that you may not want to lose. This could be time with your friends and family, passing up an opportunity or enjoying more vacation time. Whatever the case may be, you will have to make sacrifices in order to achieve your dream.

When you believe in yourself, the pathway to success is far easier to accomplish despite the hard work, failures and sacrifices you will make.

The Keys to Success

In order to understand how to achieve success, you need the tools to accomplish the task. Without the right tools, you will have a difficult time getting to where you want to go.

Possess the right work ethic.

You will have to work a little each day to achieve your dreams, even on the days you want to take off. Putting in five minutes here and ten minutes there at every opportunity puts you one step closer to making your dreams come true.

Be confident.

If you do not have the confidence to accomplish a task, then it will not get done. Building your confidence is not an overnight matter; however, it can be done if you take the time and do it right. This means starting with tasks that you can easily accomplish. One of the best ways to build your confidence is to set a short-term goal that is easily achievable and do it ahead of time, then move on to your next goal, which should be a little harder, but not too much, and proceed from there.

Success assists in building confidence, hence, it is an important tool to gradually achieving your ultimate goal.

Remove Negativity from your Life.

To succeed, you must overlook all negativity that will come from sources you may not expect. Friends and family are often the most negative to your personal success even if they do not realize it. This is because your family and friends are looking out for your best interest and do not want you to get hurt if you should falter.

Take action.

Success comes as a result of acting on laid out plans. It is not something that will come to you. This is the time you start working on important success factors decided on in the initial planning stage. This process requires a lot of energy and conscious effort, it is when you walk your talk.

Stay persistent.

You are the only person who can do it for yourself. You must believe that you can achieve all you've set out to achieve and never give up for any reason, even when you think you have a valid reason to.

However, failing is part of your success and by taking counsel of your fears by heeding the advice of friends and family, you will follow the path that leads away from your success. So, don't listen to the negative and embrace your dreams instead.

Understanding how to achieve success starts by believing in the power of self. You must keep in mind that the keys to success are within your reach. Once you know you can accomplish your dream, the next step is to plan for it to happen.

Successful people are from all walks of life with different backgrounds, education, lifestyles and locations. To be successful lies within your heart, and achieving success is something that is well within the reach of everyone. Therefore, start by taking one step at a time to make your dreams of becoming successful a reality. After all, if you believe in yourself, then anything is possible.

Believe in yourself every day!

15 Ways To Stay Motivated During Your Job Search

No feeling beats the one you have when you first start searching for a new job after college. You are excited for the future, willing to take on new challenges, and highly motivated to impress potential employers. However, when you find out that your job search is taking longer than you expected, these feelings of optimism diminish, and you begin to feel like looking for a job is a daunting task or chore. You begin to doubt your skill set with each rejection, and you also begin to question whether you're even doing the right thing. These feelings can be frustrating. The ability to stay motivated during these times is one of the most critical skills for anyone seeking a job. You have to push these feelings aside; these tips will help you do that.

1. Be realistic about the job search time frame.

You have to be realistic about the time frame of your job

search. Prepare yourself for speed bumps which are inevitable. For instance, don't expect to get an interview invite within the first week or two of starting your search.

2. Believe in yourself.

Just like a successful salesperson, you must have a strong conviction that what you are selling has value. When job hunting, you are essentially selling yourself and your skills. So, believe that you have whatever it is that the companies are looking for and need.

3. Remember why you want a job.

When you started searching for a new job, you had aspirations and things that spurred you on. After weeks of unsuccessful job searching, it is easy to lose sight of your primary motivation and focus. Maybe you wanted to pursue a career in a particular field, or you wanted new challenges. Whatever your motivation for finding a new job, don't lose sight of it. Always keep the original things that motivated you in mind and remind yourself that the dream job will eventually come, providing you don't relent and continue to work towards it. You also need to write down your career goals and even a career bucket list, if possible. You can always return to these during tough times when you are about to give up.

4. Deal with rejection constructively.

Getting rejected for a job you so desperately wanted can be frustrating, especially when you felt that the interview went well. It is natural to feel disheartened, but one thing you need to remember is never take the rejection personally. Instead, use it as an opportunity to improve yourself. Seek to know why you were rejected from the company; take what they say into serious consideration and make all the necessary amends.

5. Take time off from the job search.

The job search can sometimes seem like a job itself with all the time spent on looking for positions, completing applications and preparing for interviews. Take some time off, take a week, and focus on other aspects of your life. You can even use the time to learn a skill that will greatly add to your CV. After a short time off, you'll have renewed vigor and motivation for your job search.

6. Lean on your support network.

Do not keep your job search to yourself. Talking to friends, family and other members of your community about the progress of your job search can give you an avenue to work out your frustrations and help you see things from a different prospective. Friends and even mentors can help advise you on the jobs they feel aren't meant for you and even give you tips on how to land jobs in the future. So, open up conversations with them about your search.

7. Use online resources to keep your head in the game.

You can find your lost inspiration by just seeking online resources that are at your disposal. This could be a Ted Talk featuring someone that you look up to. By listening to them, you will let yourself be picked up by their inspirational words.

8. Don't be too hard on yourself.

Count your past achievements and remember how capable you are. In particular, remind yourself how academically sound you were in college, the skills you've been able to acquire and the amount of knowledge you have. Doing this will help you stay motivated and realize what an invaluable asset you will be to the right company.

9. Take a project-management approach.

Break down the job search process into a series of goals spread out over a period of time. For instance, you can give yourself a week to draft a resume and cover letter and another week to master interview questions and tips.

10. Keep your mind, body, and soul together.

The state of your body while job hunting can have a serious impact on your level of productivity in finding your desired job. Make sure you eat well, exercise regularly, and get enough sleep. These activities will help keep your body, mind, and soul together throughout this period.

11. Evaluate your progress.

Take some time out once in a while to assess how your job search is going. Take note of the activities you've been doing and the ones you need to start doing. Also, check to see if any of these things have been working. Improve on the activities that are working and remove those things that are not working.

12. Learn something new.

Make a conscious effort to learn something new. It can be something related to your field or just anything for fun. Learning new things has a way of stretching your brain and brightens your outlook. You can try your hand at musical instruments, like learning how to strum a few guitar chords, or you can learn a new sport.

13. Help Others.

You can take on some volunteer jobs in a company related to your field or even at a non-governmental organization (NGO). You might even make some great new contacts.

14. Read Biographies of Successful People.

Reading biographies of successful people will help you realize that every successful person encountered failures and setbacks along the way. Their stories will greatly assist you in picking yourself up and continuing your job search.

15. Get a Mentor.

If you already have a mentor, you can still get a second. You can have as many mentors as you want. These mentors will offer advice, perspective, and encouragement during your down times.

Set Up a Job Search Schedule (Daily, Weekly, Monthly)

You need to set up a job search schedule to help keep you on track in your job hunting. If you don't do this, your job hunting will only be on days you feel good, an attitude that will significantly destroy your motivation in the long run. You need to make changes to accommodate the needs of your job search. Each day you need to plan out your next day, and each week you need to plan out your next week. Make a base schedule for every day of the week, and on weekends squeeze out time to research new jobs so that on Mondays you'll have your targets ready. Your schedule should be placed on a daily calendar. Cross out each task as you complete it. You are expected to be more aggressive in the first few weeks of your job search since you are going to have more research and job listings to review. At about the third week, you should see a pattern in your routine. Below is a sample schedule.

1. *Start your day at the same time each morning* — 6:30 am will give your day a good start and keep you structured.

2. *45 minutes daily* — every morning you need to take a shower and get dressed. And not in sweat pants; you need to put on real clothing, not sleepwear. This will keep you from lying on the couch or in bed. Remember that you have to appear smart, it will make you feel good and keep you motivated.

3. *15-30 minutes daily* — eat breakfast. This is the most important meal of the day and will keep your energy levels on track.

4. *60 minutes daily* — engage in fitness training. If you usually go to the gym whether in the morning, lunch time or evenings, keep to it. Do not draw back on your fitness routine. You can take long walks or do speed walking if you don't have a fitness routine or even seek out playing your favorite sport. All these can do wonders for your fitness. Engage in workouts you can do at home; jump rope, lift weights, practice yoga and/or do sit ups. Remember to consult your fitness expert with any fitness routine you start.

5. *30 minutes daily* — review any new job listings from online search engines. Prepare a list of the jobs with their descriptions and web links.

6. *20 minutes daily* — review the classified ads and circle jobs you want to apply for.

7. *30 minutes daily* — work on your list of companies and organizations you desire to work for. Pick out a few of these companies and get the contact information of their human resource managers for the position you are applying for.

8. *20 minutes daily* — organize your list of recruiters you need to contact.

9. *30-60 minutes daily* — review your networking: leads, contacts, and LinkedIn. Make a list of jobs or companies you want to apply for. Take part in LinkedIn group discussions. Review who recently viewed your profile and try to get their contacts.

10. *60 minutes daily* — take a tea break.

11. *20 minutes twice daily* — take a 20-minute break twice daily on top of 30-60 minutes for lunch. Walk around and have snacks in-between.

12. *3-4 hours daily* — from the above list you compiled, write your cover letters and make any changes to your resume to suit each of the jobs you are applying for. Send out resumes and cover letters by mail or email and complete any online job applications. Remember, it is better to send out ten well-targeted cover letters and resumes to the right people than it is to send out 1,000 generic ones.

13. *2-3 hours weekly* — a few days during the work week, review your own finances and stay on top of them. Plan a budget and review your spending regularly. Seek money-saving avenues.

14. *2-3 hours weekly* — meet friends, colleagues, or family members for an inexpensive lunch or cup of coffee. Talk about your progress in your search; be open for advice and contacts. This will help you fight off boredom and loneliness and can also add leads to your job search.

15. *2-3 hours weekly* — fine tune your skills for landing a job. Attend seminars, online webinars, or workshops that are available to enhance your job seeking skills. Many workshops are being offered that cover skills on cover letters, resumes, looking for job openings, interview tips, time management, and so on. You can also do some research on many of these topics either online or by using books at the library or even in your local bookstore. Also, reach out to your county unemployment offices, community centers, churches, schools and colleges; many have career clubs, support groups or career services that can be very beneficial.

16. *End your job search work day at approximately 5:00 pm* — your day should end about the same time your typical work day ends, although there may be days you will need to work overtime just like in the real world of work. Spend time with friends and family, stay active and don't relegate yourself to merely lying on the couch.

17. *20 minutes daily* — before you retire to bed each evening, spend about 20 minutes checking your emails.

As you can see, a job search is a full day affair, and some things were not even included, such as job interviews, job fairs or career fairs. Maintain your routine, and if for any reason you fall out of your schedule, acknowledge it and then get back on track.

One important note, you need a workspace that is yours to use for your job search. If you have a home office space, you're in luck, but if you don't, you need to carve out space where you can work without interruptions from others.

How To Write A Cover Letter That Stands Out And Lands Job Interviews

The purpose of a cover letter is to convince the reader to read your resume and then call you for an interview. Here are some ways that will get them to do just that.

Writing a cover letter can be difficult. Many job applicants don't know how to write cover letters and as a result they fail to convert written applications to job interviews. Knowing how to write cover letters that will grab a reader's attention and maintain interest are essential job search skills.

When you apply for a job, a well written cover letter must always accompany your resume when you send it to a potential employer. Ideally, an effective cover letter should be one page, concisely written and will do the following:

- Capture the potential employer's interest.
- Explain your reason for applying for this position.
- Explain broadly how you meet the selection criteria or stated job requirements.

- State why you believe you would be the best person for the company (how you would benefit the company).
- Inspire the employer to offer you an interview.
- Your cover letter should highlight your skills and experience that address specific job requirements and show that you can do the job you are applying for. It should also contain any relevant qualifications that can support your claims.

Similarly, you need to mention aspects of your character that would benefit your prospective employers such as dependability, punctuality, motivation, problem-solving and natural leadership skills.

Your cover letter should also explain how you would fit into the organization and state your personal values that would be a good match to the image, values, and goals of the organization. To do this, however, you have to know what these are and have seriously considered how your own image, values, and goals would fit into the organization. This requires research and genuine thought.

Chances are, you have less than a minute to make a positive impression on an employer with your cover letter. This means that your cover letter must clearly and quickly get to the point. An employer quickly wants to know how you match the selection criteria, whether your written communication is of a high standard, your skills, experience and qualifications, your attention to detail, and your overall level of professionalism.

People who don't know how to write cover letters often

confuse professionalism with flowery, verbose language; even worse, words are often used in the wrong context in an effort to appear more intelligent. Needless to say, this mistake will land your application in the trash.

Cover letters should be written in plain English using formal but simple and natural language. Use positive language and avoid any mention of negative situations in previous employment. They should be printed and proofread so that there are no errors in the document. Do not indent your paragraphs; instead, use block paragraphs with a line space in between them. Make sure there are no smudges or marks on the paper.

Always address your cover letter to a real person. Never address it To Whom It May Concern or Dear Sir or Madam. If you can't find the name of the person who is going to read your cover letter any other way, you can always call and simply ask for it. If that doesn't work use Dear Employer as a last resort. It will stand out because it sounds confident.

Everyone who is applying for the job that you are seeking is also hard working, honest, and a quick learner. Don't waste your time and space telling them the obvious. Rather, explain to the reader the specific recommendations you have for opportunities or problems that you've researched, your general knowledge of the industry, or your knowledge of the company within the letter.

Keep the letter to a single page. By doing this, you are proving that you can prioritize and present your thoughts concisely, both qualities of which are admirable. In addition, it displays your respect for the busy reader, who probably has numerous resumes and cover letters to read. The letter should have a paragraph to open, 3 or 4 bullet points that are filled with only the facts, and a paragraph to close. Usually, this means about 5 or 6 paragraphs that won't exceed a single page.

After you have written your letter ask three friends for their first impressions and overall opinion, they may have advice that may be useful. Next, ask for the same thing from three people that you don't know, this feedback is valuable because they won't be worried about hurting your feelings.

A cover letter is one of the most important resources a job-seeker has. Your covering letter can make or break you. If you have a really good letter, you can get the manager to call you instantly, if your letter isn't up to the mark, it'll land in the trash. You are about to uncover some sure shot tricks to writing amazing cover letters that will make hiring managers call you instantly.

25 cover letter writing tips that will make you stand out and land an interview

Here are some tips that will help you to write effective cover letters, quickly and easily.

1. *Grab attention:* Don't start off with the usual salutations. Write a powerful headline that grabs the attention of the reader. Here's an example of a killer title:

Three Reasons Why I Believe That I May Be the Best Candidate for {Job Title}

This one tactic itself will make your cover letter amazing and will make it stand out.

2. *Begin with a proper salutation:* Do a bit of research about the company and the person to whom your letter will be arriving. If you can determine the person's name, address them directly in the letter. This personalizes the letter and also shows that you are intuitive enough to do a bit of background research on the position.

3. *Describe where you learned of the position:* Open the letter with an introductory paragraph describing where and how you learned of the position and why you are applying. Say something like, "I learned of this position from an ad in the local newspaper and am very interested in pursuing this opportunity."

4. *Be present continuous:* Don't write your letter in the past tense or in the future tense. Write your letter in the present continuous tense. Your writing tense has the power to influence the reader. If you are using the past tense or the future tense, you'll distract the reader. Write in the present continuous tense like fiction novels!

5. *Keep it short and concise:* Keep your cover letter short, less than a page. Anywhere around two to four paragraphs are excellent. Be brief in your letter and state your purpose plainly. Your purpose is to get the interview. You are going to be better off asking directly for the interview instead of bragging about your skills and work history.

6. *Sell yourself:* Give them real reasons as to why you think that you are the best man or woman for the position they are offering. Just tell them how your values relate to the company's values and goals.

7. *Avoid typos:* Avoid all typos, grammatical mistakes, etc. They'll consider you unprofessional if you leave a lot of typos on the sheet.

8. *Keep your cover letters unique:* Your cover letters have to be unique if you want to get the job. You must write a unique letter for every company you are applying to. When writing your letter, do your homework, learn everything you can about the company and include what you know about them in the letter.

9. *Send your letter to the right person:* Send your letter to the person who has the power to hire you. Don't send the letter to someone in the human resources' department, send it to the person who has the power to hire you immediately. Send a customized letter to each company you are applying for an interview.

10. *Include contact details and date:* Ensure that you include contact details and the date of writing the letter and information such as job codes given in the advertisement.

11. *Make sure you address the cover letter to the appropriate person:* If you address the incorrect person, you highlight the fact that you are not very thorough and have poor attention to detail...Would you want to employ a person like that? I didn't think so. It only takes a few minutes to call and find out the name of the recruiting person or team. Once you have that, make sure you spell it correctly.

12. *Show your prospective employer that you are seriously interested in the position:* Do this by showing them you've considered how the position fits in with your professional

goals and what you are willing to bring to the table to benefit the company you want to work for.

13. *Give a BRIEF description of your education and work experience:* Give just enough relevant information about your past work experience and your education to prove you are qualified for the position. Do not go into great detail about your alma mater as this is not the focus of your letter.

14. *Do not use the copy-paste method of sending a CVL:* Spend time actually writing a cover letter. People expect to see how specific you are about tailoring your cover letter as per the specifications of the company and job profile you are applying for, so you should make sure that comes across in your cover letter.

15. *Get details on the company:* Reading the details about the company you are applying for is a sure shot way of getting noticed. Once you mention specifically what segment of the company's existing departments can benefit from your presence and how, you will have a strong chance of being called for an interview.

16. *Do not repeat what is already mentioned in the resume:* No one has the time or patience to read the repetitive information given by hundreds of applicants. If the hiring committee feels you are wasting their time, you are sure to have your CVL trashed. Be genuine and ensure that you make the CVL interesting by showing the company the additional talents and skills you have in addition to what is already mentioned in your resume.

17. *Describe your work experience and relevant accomplishments:* This is the main portion of the letter that you want the potential employer to read. Describe your past jobs and why you were great at them. Focus on meaningful and positive changes you made in the workplace and tailor your strengths to the job announcement (i.e., do not include explanations of how you improved the copying process in your office building if you are applying for a job as a stunt man).

18. *Close with a "clincher" and your contact information:* Conclude with a paragraph telling the reader exactly what qualifies you as the best candidate for the job and why they would be remiss if they did not choose you. Include your contact information including phone number and email and explain that you would love to meet with someone to further discuss your qualifications and the specifics of the position.

19. *Minimize using the word "I":* Avoid using the word "I" too much. Restate it as "you" whenever possible. Your cover letter should be about what you can contribute to the company, not about yourself.

20. *Keep it simple:* Use Times New Roman 12 point font, short paragraphs, and bullets. Do not use italics, bold type, underlining, and so on. You want your words to stand out - not your text formatting.

21. *Use a creative closing:* Don't use the worn out "thank you for your consideration" or "Sincerely." Try something different that makes you stand out and be remembered, such as: "With my best regards" "enthusiastically yours" or "with kindest personal regards" (best for a thank you note), "good

wishes always" "Yours always."

22. *Make printed copies attractive:* For paper copies of your cover letter (and resume), use good quality stationary and a good quality printer. This is the first impression you'll make, so be sure it's a professional one.

23. *Avoid generalities:* Avoid using ready-made phrases such as "self-starter," "proven leadership skills," "excellent inter-personal skills," and so on, unless you have specific examples of accomplishments to back them up. Otherwise, you come across as throwing around today's buzz words with nothing substantial to back them up.

24. *Don't exaggerate:* Never overstate your experience or skills when you write a cover letter. If you aren't found out in the interview, you certainly will be if you get the job. Even if you don't have every qualification listed in a job ad, be honest about yourself and highlight your strengths.

25. *Have someone else proofread:* Finally, have someone else you trust read your cover letter for spelling, punctuation and grammatical errors. You can read your own letter ten times and not spot an obvious error that someone else sees immediately. Don't let that someone else be the hiring manager.

Understanding how to write a cover letter for a resume is key to grabbing your prospective employer's attention and causing them to want to go through your resume with detail. Follow the steps outlined above and you will increase your chances of getting the job you want.

Writing a Cover Letter Introduction

When it comes to cover letters, the days of the default introduction are officially over—and they have been for quite some time. In our modern value-driven workplace, make your individual merit clear from the very first sentence of your cover letter. Grab the hiring manager's attention and hold it. Start by addressing the hiring manager by name (no more "Dear Sir/ Madame" it smacks of disinterest and a lack of research) and end with a concise, action-oriented pitch. Vague, rambling, and formulaic cover letters need not apply.

Alas, with pre-interview jitters fogging your mind, accomplishing the above can feel like a Herculean effort. Fortunately, we're here to help. To get your creative juices flowing and provide you with structural and stylistic cues, we've come up with the following ten eye-catching cover letter introduction examples:

#1: Assuming that loving data is not right, I would prefer to be wrong. Seemingly, other members of the team at Woopra have similar feelings – and this is why I would be the most suitable candidate for this job.

#2: Being a recent graduate of computer science and an applicant for the position of an Android developer, I am coming into this position with passion, commitment, and desire. With my readiness to put to use what I have learned to improve my career, I have no doubt about the suitability of my skill and experience for this position as an Android app developer.

#3: Having seen the relevance of my qualifications to your listing for the position of an HR Assistant, I am using this opportunity to show my passion and interest in working for you. Since the completion of my business degree from the University of Quebec–Montreal in May, I enrolled to improve my knowledge of HR strategies through a human resource development program.

#4: When I was seven, I wanted to be the GEICO gecko when I grew up. I eventually realized that wasn't an option, but you can imagine my excitement when I came across the events manager position, which would have me working side by side with my favorite company mascot.

#5: These days, recent graduates are usually told to "Just get a job—any job." We're taught to wait around for the right opportunity to come along, one that will allow us to finally leverage our skills and passion. Personally, I don't agree. I think the first steps we take set the tone for the rest of our career journey. That's why I want to embrace the opportunities for mentorship, professional development, and excellence that I know Shareco will provide.

#6: I am a marketing graduate from Imperial College in Australia, with experience in managing groups and facilitating communication. I am participating in a twelve month USA Work Visa Program, which allows me to take a job in the US for up to a year. I have a US Sponsor and authorized work papers which will commence on March 30th, and I would appreciate an opportunity to interview for a relevant internship or a job opening with your company.

#7: Most candidates are drawn to startups for the free food, bean bag chairs, and free dress code. And while all of those things sound awesome coming from my all-too-corporate cubicle, what really attracted me to Factual is the collaborative, international team.

#8: Thank you for allowing me to present myself as a candidate for the position of Music Instructor, a prospect about which I am very excited. Given my background, I can understand the need for an instructor who maintains a working knowledge of the industry and can effectively transfer that knowledge to students through comprehensive instruction and hands-on experience. What this means for you is that as a Music Instructor, I can bring the skill, insight, and expertise to motivate students in the classroom.

#9: When I was growing up, all I wanted to be was one of those people who pretend to be statues on the street. Thankfully, my career goals have become a little more aspirational over the years, but I love to draw a crowd and entertain the masses—passions that make me the perfect community manager.

#10: The other day, I took a career assessment, which told me I should be a maritime merchant. I'm not quite sure what that is, but it did get me thinking: A role that combines my skills in business development with my lifelong passion for the ocean would be my absolute dream. And this is how I found this position at Royal Caribbean.

The Secret to Writing the Perfect Cover Letter Introduction

Before you begin writing your cover letter introduction, you should take a few minutes to analyze what makes the ten examples above so efficient. To stand out, each introduction above contains one or more of the following elements:

A clear passion for the company offering the job

While you don't want to come off like you're overtly trying to flatter the company you're applying to, an authentic demonstration of appreciation never goes amiss.

At least one mention of a job-specific skill

This clearly tells the hiring manager why they should keep reading—and pay attention. It also helps to immediately differentiate you from the many other qualified candidates that are probably applying for the position.

Humor

Humor does more than just give the hiring manager a chuckle; it also demonstrates the fact that you have great creative thinking and communication skills. Note, however, that you shouldn't joke around on your cover letter simply for the sake of it; any piece of humor you use should be job (and industry) specific. Ideally, you should also make sure that it's the kind of humor that will make you look like a good fit for the company's culture.

Storytelling

Everyone—hiring managers included—likes to hear an engaging story. Storytelling illustrates your personal interest in the position being offered while also showing off your unique communication style. Likewise, using storytelling as a stylistic device on your cover letter will help the hiring manager feel like they are making a personal connection with you. This will ensure that you stick out in their memory.

Brevity

A good cover letter introduction will get to the point, fast. Remember that the hiring manager has probably already flipped through a stack of cover letters; they are tired, bored, and their attention span is wearing thin. Don't waste time beating around the bush: Use concise, action-oriented language and dive right into explaining why you're an excellent candidate.

5 Step surefire formula on how to write a cover letter that will land a job interview

Here is the 5 Step Cover Letter Writing Formula:

1. *Identify Industry Specific Problem:* Hiring managers look for problem-solvers. What problem would hiring you solve?

2. *Write an Attention Getting Introduction:* Make an emotional connection.

3. *Be Conversational and Personal:* Address the name of the Hiring Manager (never send a To Whom It May Concern or a Dear Sir or Madam cover letter).

4. *Provide a Solution:* Include 3-4 benefits driven bullet points–Answer the What's In It For Me Question (for the hiring manager)

5. *Ask for the Job Interview:* Close the cover letter with a very strong call to action. Request an interview.

Top ten cover letter writing mistakes to avoid

Your cover letter shows recruiters how well you can express yourself. It also demonstrates how savvy you are regarding marketing and selling yourself and your skills. A good cover letter can woo a recruiter into reviewing your resume. A bad cover letter, on the other hand, can stall your chances. Here are ten mistakes you need to avoid when writing cover letters:

1. *Failing to be specific in addressing the letter:* using generic words like "Dear Personnel Manager", "To Whom It May Concern", "Dear Sir or Ma'am" are all bad ways of addressing a cover letter and it shows an employer that you are not concerned enough to inquire about the name of the person with the hiring power. Finding the name of the particular person with the hiring power may not always be easy, but you must try to get their name. You can always do this by just calling the company to inquire who the hiring manager is for a particular position. Tap into your professional network to learn the names of HR managers. You can ask someone who works in the company for the names of the hiring personnel if the company posts a listing. You can also use the internet to track down the names of hiring managers. Once you've found the precise name of the hiring personnel, address your cover letter to them.

2. *Sending your resume without a cover letter:* although some recruiters don't read or place much value on cover letters, you

still have to include a cover letter with every resume you're sending as you wouldn't know the employer that would want to see it.

3. *Telling the recruiter what the company can do for you instead of what you can do for the company:* this mistake mainly applies to fresh college graduates. Every employer is in business to make a profit, so they would want to know how you are going to help them make this profit. In writing your cover letter, state how you are going to help the company with your skills to achieve their aims; not how you want them to help you fulfill your career dreams.

4. *Not including a strong call to action:* lines like "I look forward to hearing from you" are vague ways of ending a cover letter and doesn't send any serious message. Make use of strong call to action words to request for interviews. Come right out and ask for an interview, don't be vague about it. You can take it a step further by telling the recruiter that you will contact them in a specific period of time to arrange for an interview appointment. And if you say that you'll follow up, do so. If you take this proactive approach, the odds will seriously be in your favor regarding getting interviews. This follow-up is yet another reason why you need the specific names of the hiring managers. Here is a sample closing paragraph requesting and describing the writer's planned follow-up. "I would like to be considered for a sales position in which someone of my background could make a contribution. I will contact you to arrange for an interview. Should you require any additional information, feel free to contact me using the phone numbers listed above."

5. *Writing a boring introduction:* your introduction is your opportunity to wow the employer and grab his attention. Don't waste it on irrelevancies. Check the section on writing cover letter introductions to avoid mistakes when writing your introduction. Tell the recruiter why you are writing and summarize the reasons that make you qualified for the job, expanding on your qualifications in subsequent paragraphs.

6. *Allowing misspellings, typos, incorrect grammar or punctuation in your letter:* your letter reflects communication and literary abilities. In writing your cover letter, make sure you don't misspell words and that your sentences are grammatically correct. Before sending it out, proofread to correct all errors. You can engage a friend to help as well.

7. *Rehashing your resume:* aspects of your resume that are relevant to the position you are applying can be highlighted in your cover letter but don't be tempted to repeat your resume in the cover letter as that will simply amount to a waste of precious space.

8. *Failing to tailor your letter to the specific position you're applying for:* if you are answering an online job listing or ad, the contents of your letter should tally as closely as possible with the actual words of the listing you're answering. In responding to ads, echo the authors' intent and words, and also flatter the person who wrote the listing with your letter. Your letter should be a mirror of the ad.

9. *Revealing too much:* your letter should be as brief as possible. It should be one page at most. Keeping your letter to four or five paragraphs of no more than 50 to 60 words each is a

good guideline. Using bullet points in the letter is a good way of showcasing yourself to the reader. Some job-seekers often tend to use their cover letters to narrate the stories of their life or career. That's clearly a misuse of the letter; it's a marketing tool that should focus on the qualifications that will sell you to the employer. Your letter should answer the question that the company will be asking while reading the words you've written: "Why should I hire this person?" Answer with your Unique Selling Proposition. Use simple language and simple sentence structure too. Avoid using all unnecessary words.

10. *Using wimpy language:* don't use such phrases as "I believe" and "I think." They show uncertainty. Your statements will convey stronger messages without them. It's best to either use a strong qualifier or leave off the qualifier entirely. Active qualifiers such as "I am positive," I am convinced," or "I am confident" should be used.

CHAPTER 4

25 Resume Writing Tips That Will Get You Hired

Your resume is the most important part of your job application. It is the first document that prospective employers see, and if they are not impressed, they probably will not see the rest of your job application. A quality resume could be the decisive factor in the success of your job search. In this case, you cannot afford to show potential employers a poorly formatted and visually unappealing listing of your experience and skills.

On first look, there are some things the recruiter would want to see on a resume. These are the things that increase your chances of reaching the next step of the recruitment exercise. The job of a recruiter is much simpler than you think. Just check if a candidate seems to have the chance to be a good match for the advertised role. If so, go to the next step. Otherwise, they reject. Below is basically how recruiters absorb resumes. Recruiters spend on average just six seconds skimming through a resume before deciding if the candidate

35

is worth calling for an interview. The following are 24 resume writing tips that will surely get you hired:

1. Organize your resume properly.

In listing your qualifications, skills, and achievements, do so in a reverse chronological order. The most recent skills, achievements or experiences should come first before the older ones. Your resume must be clearly organized. A typical chronological resume should have the following sections:

- Contact details
- Professional Summary
- Work experience
- Education
- Publications
- Skills / Qualifications
- Certifications / Awards
- References

2. Don't put everything on there.

If you have a lot of skills you've acquired in the course of your college study, be sure to pick out the best, the most relevant and the most important. Leave out the ones that are not related to the current job you are applying for.

3. It is best to use a one-page resume.

The one page versus the two-page resume is an issue that has generated heated argument over the years. But an argument for a one-page resume is that one page is just enough to provide a brief presentation of your skills and experiences. In instances where you can't squeeze everything into one page, then you can use two pages, but that should be the limit.

4. Limit your use of bullet points.

Yes, using bullet points on your resume is a great way of passing a piece of information quickly and efficiently. But as with other things, you have to strike a balance in your use of bullet points. Don't overuse them but don't underuse them either. Limit your use of bullet points to about five or six and don't forget to start with the important and impressive points first.

5. Quantify your achievements.

Using actual statistics and numbers is an excellent persuasion tactic. If there are past achievements you've made, it's better to state the real statistic than just being vague. Example, it's better to say "I managed a team of 10 software developers" than just saying "I managed a small team of developers."

6. Don't forget keywords.

Welcome to the 21st century. Large and even medium sized companies now use the applicant tracking system (ATS) to meet hundreds, if not thousands, of candidates who apply for the same positions everyday. This resume reading software allows these companies to automate, streamline and manage the hiring process.

Why do companies allow robots to make human resource

decisions? The answer is that they are trying to speed up the process.

Going through resumes to select candidates is a tedious job. And as you know, recruiters have to go through thousands of resumes at some point. But ATS streamlines this process by identifying candidates whose resumes contain valuable experience and skills that match the qualifications being sought by employers. So including the keywords that appear in the job listing on your resume will no doubt make it stand apart from all the other resumes they have on file.

7. Include only relevant competencies.

Include only those skills that are pertinent to the job you are applying for. Simply declaring all your skills will not get the attention of a recruiter, so be sure to explain how your skills make you the best match for the job.

8. Personalize your resume for each job.

The most common mistake made by job seekers is to create a generic resume and send it to all jobs. Personalize your resume for each job application. Make sure your resume has keywords that the recruiter is looking for.

9. Include only relevant work experience.

Desist from listing unrelated job experiences on your resume. If you are applying for a software developer position, including your part-time job as a car mechanic adds no value to your resume.

10. Never lie on your resume.

Never tell a lie on your resume. If you have no relevant work experience, include your summer internship or volunteer work experience; if you do not have a college degree then mention all the non-credit courses that you have taken. Whatever you do, just do not lie on your resume.

11. Ask someone else to proofread your resume.

Even if you think your resume seems okay, it would be a good idea to get a second and third opinion on it. Usually, we become blind to our mistakes or mode of reasoning. Because of this, other people will be in a better position to assess the overall quality of your resume and make appropriate suggestions.

12. Keep your resume up to date.

Make sure your resume is kept up to date. Continue to add courses, certifications or volunteer work on a regular basis. This can save you from having to send an obsolete resume to an employer.

13. Do not blindly copy resume sample templates.

There are many sample resumes available online. If you use a sample CV, make sure you make the appropriate changes.

14. Use appropriate blank spaces.

Make sure your resume is readable and well-spaced. A resume stuffed with too many words is almost impossible to read. Similarly, a resume with a lot of space and few words seems fragile and unimportant. Your goal should be to have a good mix of white space and words.

15. Use consistent line spacing.

Be consistent in the use of line spacing. It is recommended that you use a double space between the headers and body text and a single space in the subtitles.

16. Use coherent vertical alignment.

To purge the text, make sure your vertical alignment is consistent. Use tabs or spaces. Having a mix of tabs or spaces in different sections can ruin the appearance of a well-written resume.

17. Make your resume clear, concise and to the point.

Human resource managers spend an average of 6 seconds scanning a resume and can throw your resume away if you are too vague. Make sure your resume is concise and relevant. Avoid including irrelevant information. Organize your information so that the most important points are easily visible.

18. Use effective job titles.

Since you have about 6 seconds to show your skills and accomplishments to your potential employer, make sure your titles stand out. Try to be as descriptive and eye-catching as possible.

19. Write a focused profile section.

Include a targeted and effective profile section. This section should be such that it catches the attention of readers. Use this section to indicate what you hope to do for the company. It is best to use a bulleted list.

20. Correct at least twice.

It is difficult to overestimate the importance of reviewing your resume. Read your resume twice and look for common spelling mistakes or grammatical errors. Also, get help from a friend, if possible.

21. Show your achievements rather than responsibilities.

In the Experience section, highlight your accomplishments and achievements rather than listing your duties and responsibilities. In addition, whenever possible, present your work experience as challenges or resolved problems. A recruiter already knows the job responsibilities but would be more interested in what you did in your previous job.

22. Avoid unnecessary information.

Information such as ethnicity, marital status, and religious beliefs should not be included in your resume. Avoid fluffy statements such as "I'm well organized and pay attention to details." Also, avoid using statements like "References available upon request."

23. Prioritize the content of your resume.

When you order your resume sections and items within each section, make sure that the important section is presented first. Prioritize your statements in order of importance, relevance, and impressiveness.

24. Use italic and bold font to add accent.

Moderately use italic and boldface to make some sections more obvious. Do not underline text, it makes your resume lose some of its visual clarity.

Top Ten Resume Writing Mistakes to Avoid

Increase your chances of impressing a potential employer by avoiding the following 10 mistakes when writing your resume:

1. *A lengthy resume:* You should show off your ability to summarize points in your resume. One page is an ideal resume for a fresh college graduate. Don't be tempted to add unnecessary information that will likely put your potential employer off. Avoid the use of cliché words like passionate, hardworking and motivated. Get to the point and show an employer why he or she should choose you above the others.

2. *Avoid writing in continuous prose style:* what you should do instead is to write in snippets. Paragraphs should be kept short and precise. Long paragraphs, especially in your summary section, will often be ignored by recruiters. You don't need to write full sentences in your resume. Your reader will basically be skimming through; hence, write in a news flash

pattern. Try an "action result" format to make important points stand out. An example of an action result you can use in your resume is: "proposed cost-cutting plan, shaving 10% off budget". This is better than just saying "I proposed a cost-cutting plan."

3. *Being too generic:* Your resume should be tailored to each position you are applying for. Though there may be roles with similar requirements, they will still be different in some aspects. Read each job description carefully and make sure you understand all the requirements. Write your resume to target those requirements. Be ready to move sections and details around to put the spotlight on different information. If an important requirement is a particular grade, put that prominently in your profile.

4. *Lacking the "so what" factor:* You need to ensure that there is a clear connection between what you write and what your potential employer wants to see. Point out the connection between your education and the requirements of the job. Find the business value of your degree or other skills you have. What are the things you can do with these experiences? How will that be useful in the job you are seeking? For instance, a project or course module might be of value to an employer. Useful phrases like "trained to" should be used to buttress your competencies. For example, if you have a business studies degree, you could say: "trained to analyze complex data and identify the greatest return on investment." Or if you have an arts degree for roles where good communication skills are important, you could say: "trained to research, summarize and

present key findings clearly and concisely." Your resume is in competition with other people's resumes, so make it relevant and address each specific job requirement.

5. *Not selling your achievements:* Find and highlight achievements you made in the course of your study. It could be leading a small project team in school or something similar. We often tend to shy away from highlighting our successes, but put yourself in the shoes of your potential employer and give them what they want, without necessarily crossing the line into arrogance.

You have to understand what's important in the role so that you can match your examples. For businesses, achievements typically fall into three categories: decreasing costs, increasing profits, and streamlining processes. But depending on the type of organization, you might need to prove success in other relevant areas, such as creating successful work teams to deliver products or services within a tight budget.

6. *Underestimating other experiences:* Though there is a need for you to be selective about what you add to your resume, don't underestimate your experiences by excluding the details of more humble roles, voluntary jobs, or outside activities. If you were once the president of a club or society, it could be worth adding if under your leadership your club or society achieved something great. Don't neglect experience that will prove you have those difficult-to-quantify character traits that graduate employers like to see, such as showing that you're hard-working and have teamwork skills.

7. *Wooly vocabulary:* Employers can sometimes be guilty of

filling their job descriptions with vague words. These vague wordings shouldn't, by any means, find their way into your resume as it looks unsubstantiated. It is good to think that you are an innovative problem solver, or that you are passionate about working in the sector; nonetheless, you should have examples to show those qualities. Quantify your achievements using numbered lists and short narratives to show your qualities in action.

8. *Dull language:* Phrases like "duties included" and "responsible for" are passion killers in a resume. Use powerful action verbs to wet a potential employer's appetite. Spice up your resume with action verbs at the beginning of sentences. "Increased app store ranking by 10%." Cut out wordiness and avoid using passive forms or too much background information.

9. *Unnecessary details:* When describing many past responsibilities, the day-to-day details are often unnecessary and take up space. Concentrate on the highlights and where you made an impact. If you had a summer job working in a cafe, the duties are easily predictable and don't need to be on your resume. What's of more interest is how many people you served per shift, whether you were entrusted to take payments, and so on.

Sometimes, however, you need context. For example, you might need to include key data on the companies you worked with to give an idea of the scope of your role. Experiment by putting this in a smaller font under the company name, so you have more room for the interesting details.

10. *Lacking keywords:* If you're applying online, your resume will probably need to contain the right keywords before getting through to the next stage. Keywords are job-specific phrases and terminology that can include particular qualifications or areas of expertise. Check the job description to identify what these are and make sure you include them as appropriate points in your resume.

CHAPTER 5

25 Job Search Strategies Every College Graduate Should Know

When it comes to your job search as a recent college graduate, there are a lot of strategies you should know and employ to ensure you get a job after college within your chosen industry.

Complete the following job search exercise, it will help you gain focus and clarity in your search.

1. Compile a list of target companies you want to work for.

If there's one thing you don't want to be doing, it's stabbing in the dark for job opportunities. Don't sit and wait around for "any" company to notice you on LinkedIn or the recruitment sites you subscribe to. Make a list of the companies you want to work for most and aim for those organizations.

2. Research your targeted companies.

Once you've decided who you want to work for, get busy researching everything you need to know about them. Who occupies positions of high authority in the company? What has the company recently contributed to your industry? What kind of company culture do they have?

3. Identify a problem the company has and prepare to explain how you can help them solve it.

Remember, getting a job is all about conveying the *value* you can add to the company. Talking about your qualifications is not enough; think about how you can use them to solve a problem the organization is facing.

Here, we present some of these job search strategies:

1. *Sign up for Google Alerts to keep abreast of the companies you want to be employed by.* Google Alerts can be an excellent ally when it comes to your job search. Google alerts are notifications you get from Google that monitor the internet for new information about a particular topic of interest. Conducting your daily manual searches can never be as efficient as using the watchful eye of the largest search engine in the world. Google Alerts are also a great tool to get ideas for writing articles as a content marketing strategy for your job search.

For a fresh college graduate, you can use Google Alerts in three ways:

- To get notified of new positions that become open,
- To monitor your online reputation, and
- To stay updated on news from your target companies.

It is therefore critical, as a recent college graduate, that you know how to sign up for Google Alerts; it will help you stay on top of things in your job search. Google Alerts can make you look sharp to a prospective employer.

2. *Leverage the power of professional social networks.* Create a LinkedIn account, write articles related to your industry and submit them on LinkedIn, using LinkedIn Pulse, an article submission tool. Sharing relevant industry information with hiring managers and recruiters is a very powerful way to show your expertise and knowledge. These professional social networks are the fastest growing sources of quality hire globally. Recent research shows that LinkedIn has increased by more than 73 percent in the past four years. As a recent college graduate, getting ahead of this trend could be very beneficial.

LinkedIn stands out among all of the professional networks available today. It operates the world's largest professional social network on the internet with over 364 million members in more than 200 countries. It hosts recruiters, job hunters, employers and other professionals from all over the world. As a fresh college graduate, one of the first things you should know is how to leverage the opportunities inherent in LinkedIn.

3. *Create a killer LinkedIn summary.* As a college graduate, you should know how to create a killer LinkedIn summary. First impressions count, and your LinkedIn summary is the first opportunity a potential employer has to find out who you are beyond your photo and title. Always use industry keywords when you create your LinkedIn summary.

4. *Create an excellent LinkedIn profile.* As a recent college graduate, it's important to have a resume that is up to date

and have a LinkedIn profile that is optimized with industry keywords to make you findable on LinkedIn by hiring managers and recruiters. It is something that is worth learning as it can help open doors and alert you to new opportunities if you follow all the necessary steps to create a killer profile.

5. *Build your own personal branding website.* If you have your own personal branding website, you can always showcase your works there and include a link to your website on any application you are sending. Creating a personal website is no longer hard, as there are online tools like WordPress and Blogger that can help you create a personal branding website in a few minutes. This is something that you really need to know how to do.

6. *Write a resume.* Writing a resume isn't just the issue we are talking about here, but writing a winning resume that will land you an interview. Chapter 4 of this book is dedicated to writing resumes; use it to learn all the intricacies of writing a winning resume as it is one of the things you are expected to know.

7. *Write a cover letter.* Just like the resume, you also need to know how to write a good cover letter. Chapter 3 is dedicated exclusively to writing cover letters, use it to learn everything you need to know.

8. *Learn how to network properly.* College students and recent graduates are sometimes not adept to face-to-face networking. Even online networking can be challenging. As a college graduate, you have a lot to learn about using face-to-face networking to broaden your professional networks.

9. *Know hot industry topics that will be relevant for interviewing.* You will soon start attending interviews, and it is necessary that you know hot industry trends that are related to your field that are worth interviewing. Knowing these hot topics will help you ace most of your interviews.

10. *Know how to use keywords to keep abreast of industry trends.* You can do this by subscribing to keywords within your area of specialization. Examples of keywords include "change management" and "effective leadership". As a graduate, you need to know to how to set up specific alerts for your particular industry to keep you abreast of current information.

11. *Attend seminars and conferences.* There are various seminars and conferences you can attend that can help with your job search. If you can't make it to conferences, scan the session's descriptions and programs. You can always find these online. From there, you can find leads to further investigate.

12. *Scout out forums for your profession.* Forums for your profession can also be a good place to get connected with people that can hire you. The groups and discussions features on LinkedIn are a great place to start.

13. *Pay attention to what the top bloggers in your area of expertise are writing about.* You don't have to always take their words or agree with them; however, knowing other people's perspective is often insightful.

14. *Attend online webinars.* Many webinars are free, so leverage that to learn new things in your profession as well as to network.

15. *Be versatile with basic computer programs.* Consider

taking a class or learn to use them on your own. A few basic computer programs to learn are Excel, Word, PowerPoint, Microsoft Access, Spreadsheets, and QuickBooks.

16. *Subscribe to newsletters.* Most consulting firms, educational institutions, authors, and experts have a newsletter or mailing list. Stay up to date by subscribing to newsletters that consistently put out innovative, interesting, and substantive information.

17. *Leverage the power of content marketing.* Using relevant keywords and catchy titles for your articles will give them more exposure as well as showcase your industry knowledge to recruiters and hiring managers. Go to the Google Keyword Tool and research the monthly search volume of keywords related to your industry. Write your articles using keywords in the article titles that will attract the attention of hiring managers, recruiters and professionals in your industry. Here is an example of an article title: "Top Ten Skills of a First Time Manager". Write articles 600-1000 words and always have your contact information at the end of every article. This is also called a Resource Box. Having a Personal Branding website or blog makes this a very powerful job search strategy. You can put your Personal Branding website on your resume and cover letter. Through SEO (search engine optimization), it becomes easier for people to get access to your articles on the web. While creating articles, start the titles of the articles with keywords such as "top ten", "10 ways", "10 keys", "10 steps" and the like will help increase the probability of Internet users to click on your contents. Similarly, the headlines of your

articles need to be appealing in order to capture the attention of the readers; as the headline is the first impression of the article to the reader – and would determine if they should continue reading or not.

In addition to these, you need to know how to develop your soft skills continuously. Knowing how to manage yourself and lead other people is an ever evolving art.

18. *Focus on popular job search sites and use relevant job search keywords.* As a college graduate hunting for jobs, you should focus your time and effort more on those job search sites used by the majority of companies to increase your chances of finding relevant job openings related to your industry. If possible, visit the website of the company you want to apply. Job search engines like After College and LinkUp, can be a great tool for searching for jobs online. They have features that allow you to search for job openings directly from company websites including an advanced search feature that drills down job postings to the barest relevant minimum.

19. *Do not stop or limit your job search to the Internet.* Tell as many people you know that you are looking for a job. Unless you want to continue searching for jobs for a long time, you need to leave the comfort of your computer and home and go out. After applying for a job online, it may be necessary that you follow up by meeting people who work at the place where you applied. Establishing contact with a staff member or someone in the company can be important; you can meet with an internal recruiter or HR personnel and ask questions about the company and about your job application. This can

make you endearing to them as well as increase your chances of getting the job.

20. *Create social media accounts and join social media groups related to your industry.* There are many groups on social media platforms like Facebook, Twitter, Meetup and others where job seekers can meet, discuss and share information. These social media groups are a great way to share your articles or any other information that will showcase your industry knowledge. While searching for a group to join, you should ensure that the group is related to your career/industry in order not to waste your time. Through these groups, you can connect and network with like-minded people who may help you with your job search.

21. *Create a YouTube video and Slideshare presentation.* Use content from an existing article that you have written and repurpose it into a YouTube video and Slideshare presentation. Use the same article title and keywords that you used in your article. You can also create a short "how to" YouTube or Slideshare presentation that will educate your industry/target audience. Share that same video and presentation on your social media accounts and social media groups.

22. *Publish articles on article directories.* With the development of the web, it is now easy to have almost anything posted on the Internet. You can use this to your advantage. Write and publish academic-related articles on websites like Buzzfeed or Medium, and on other article directory websites such as ehow.com, hubpages.com, etc. Submitting your articles on these platforms will increase the exposure of your articles to

larger audiences and ultimately give you exposure. However, ensure that the articles are education-based.

23. *Schedule informational interviews.* According to the University of Berkeley Career Center, an informational interview is "An informal conversation with someone working in an area that interests you who can give you information and advice." Informational interviews are both an excellent way to prepare for real job interviews and an effective research tool. To schedule one, reach out to senior employees in your field and ask if they'd be willing to talk to you.

24. *Network in "real life" too.* College grads raised in the digital era sometimes fail to realize that "face to face" interaction is as important as connecting online. Use services like Eventbrite to find industry-related events in your area. As an alternative, create one of your own.

25. *Practice for job interviews.* Practice, plan and prepare for job interviews. Your goal is to stand out in job interviews and become the irresistible "hire". Study the interview questions and answers in this book and do mock interviews with your friends and family so you will ace your job interviews and get hired for jobs.

Once you have mastered the 25 Job Search Strategies above, there will be no trouble in drawing the attention of hiring managers and recruiters to yourself. Follow up on these tips and others found in this book by learning how to interview well, and it's almost guaranteed that you'll land an exciting position in your industry soon.

CHAPTER 6

25 Job Interview Tips That Will Help You Land A Job

Interviews can be tricky at times even for the most experienced job seekers. Nevertheless, there are a few tips you can use to scale through that interview and land your dream job. Here we provide 25 of these tips.

1. Be a problem solver.

The ability to look at a problem and devise solutions that are efficient and innovative is a desirable trait to a hiring manager. Demonstrate this early on in the way you craft your resume, drawing attention to projects you've worked on where problem-solving was required, and substantiate this perception further in an interview setting.

2. Conduct research.

Thoroughly research your potential employer. The more you know about them, the better. Know about the founders of the company, their headquarters, their mission statement and any other relevant information about the company as you may be asked about that.

3. Review common interview questions.

Take some time to practice some common interview questions so that you can better prepare for your actual interview.

4. Practice.

Once you've gotten all of the relevant information you need, practice answering and asking questions until you become conversant with them. Try to memorize some key talking points and reply to them.

5. Dress smart.

Show up for the interview looking smart to increase your chances of landing the job. Remember what they say about dressing as you'd want to be addressed.

6. Be punctual: When it comes to job interviews, punctuality should be your best friend. Try to show up a few minutes early. But don't enter the office any more than 15 minutes early.

7. Make a great first impression.

Remember what they say about not always having a second chance to make a first impression. So from the moment you get into the office, create good first impressions. Words get around. Everybody at the company deserves your respect so be mindful of every conversation you have.

8. Stay calm and calculated.

Even if you're nervous, which is totally normal, don't let it show. The calmer you are, the more your preparations will pay off. Try perfecting power poses before entering the office. Research shows that by making your body big, you will feel more self-assured and confident.

9. Show what you know.

Companies like it when prospective members of the company know about the company. Show all the research you've done on the company, but be careful not to make glaring mistakes. If you tell the CEO that his company's stocks have dropped, when it actually doubled, you're not likely making a great impression.

10. Be unique.

The company is looking to hire you for who you are, not the person you may pretend to be. So be yourself, or rather a more polished version of yourself.

11. Mind your body language.

Apart from the words you say, your disposition also conveys messages. Sit up straight and take up space in your chair. The more you cross your legs or unconsciously make yourself small, the more insecure you appear.

12. Maintain eye contact.

Show your confidence by maintaining eye contact all

through the interview. If it is a panel interview, first address the interviewer asking the questions before moving between the other interviewers for 4-5 seconds at a time. If need be, practice with friends beforehand.

13. Emphasize your good qualities.

Ensure you highlight all of your good qualities to show the interviewers what you can offer the company.

14. Be humble, not arrogant.

Having a lot of confidence is good, but arrogance is a total turn off. Some interviewers may take your arrogance seriously though you are just trying to come across as casual.

15. Don't brag.

Bragging as with arrogance can make you appear unprofessional. Highlight your success but with humility.

16. Be honest.

Never lie about your weaknesses or strengths. You can, however, find a way to frame your weaknesses to show that you can acknowledge them, but plan on improving them.

17. Be concise.

Don't bore the interviewer with irrelevancies. Go straight and hit your points. A good rule of thumb is to try to keep all answers to two sentences at most.

18. Use appropriate language.

You're in a professional environment and not hanging out with some casual friends. So choose your words wisely. Refrain from coming across as overly familiar with your interviewers no matter how comfortable the company's culture may appear.

19. Listen.

Interviewers feed you with a lot of direct and indirect information. Pay attention and use that information to your advantage. Your interviewers may feel disrespected if you are interrupting or turning the conversation to yourself.

20. Don't appear desperate.

Rather than appearing desperate, make it look as if you are passionate about the job. Use phrases like "Based on X, this seems like a good match to me. I feel that I would bring Y to the table, and I think that Company Z would be a great next step."

21. Give specific examples.

For each question your interviewer throws at you, give a specific example. Rather than saying things like "I increased productivity in our new system," name the things you did. For example, you can say "I led my team to carry out a system analysis and design of a new system that helped our organization increase productivity by 10%."

22. Ask important questions.

Always prepare a few questions to ask your interviewer as a way of showing your interests. But be sure that you adapt each question to the flow of your interviewer. Don't ask irrelevant questions that have been addressed before in the course of the interview.

23. Refer to your interviewers by name.

This helps establish a personal relationship that goes a long way. You can also work to find areas of common interest. It could be you attending the same high school or having a common acquaintance. Any shared interest can help your interviewers relate to you better, creating a lasting impression.

24. Follow up.

After your interview, send a thank you email to stay at the top of your interviewers' mind. And if you discussed any common interests during the interview, you may hint at it. But do this only in situations where it seems useful not for common topics.

25. Find out why you weren't hired.

If you don't land the job, find out the reasons so you can improve for your next interview. Some employers will be happy to offer feedback which can help you prepare for your next interview.

15 Interview Skills That Will Get You Hired

In competing with so many applicants for any given job and throughout the hiring process, what does a hiring manager look for which will differentiate you from other job candidates?

1. Knowledge of the Company

In the same way a hiring manager is interviewing you and investing in getting to know you, and whether or not you're a good fit for their company, a hiring manager is also looking to see if you've also done your homework. Take the time to research the companies you are applying to work for, including their strengths and weaknesses; and demonstrate this by asking intelligent questions about the company.

2. Problem Solver

The ability to look at a problem and devise solutions that are efficient and innovative is a desirable skill to a hiring manager. Demonstrate this early on in the way you craft your resume, drawing attention to projects you've worked on where problem-solving was required, and substantiate this perception further in an interview setting.

3. Great Attitude

Most people do not like to work with or hire a grouch. Put on a smile, develop an authentic "can do" attitude, and let this shine through when you interact with hiring managers. Remember, if the hiring manager doesn't enjoy being around you and your attitude, they can be fairly sure your would-be co-workers also wouldn't enjoy you, and you probably won't make the cut.

4. Team Player

Employers are interested in hiring those who work well with others and who recognize that greatness is never achieved in a silo. Demonstrating that you are a team player to a prospective employer is powerful. As you share your past work experiences, demonstrate your ability to work in a team by highlighting the strengths of the teams you've worked on in the past and praise others for their contributions in addition to mentioning your own.

5. Flexibility

Employers want to hire professionals who can flex. A person who is stuck in their ways and doesn't demonstrate adaptability tends to be harder to work with. This is especially important in today's corporate climate where job scopes change and evolve day by day to meet a company's needs. Employers know they can get more mileage out of a professional who can adapt to a variety of job requirements and company needs.

6. Growth Mindset

This is perhaps the most misunderstood and yet the most important skill that will affect the impression you leave with a hiring manager. A growth mindset is not meant to indicate you are a professional intent on growth within an organization, upward mobility, and a desire to advance in your position. Rather, a growth mindset means you look at your job, your company and your work responsibilities with the eye of someone intent on personal growth and development. You are a professional who will continue learning, perfecting your skills and learning new ones, and someone who is agile and capable of growth and change. You may have held the same position for ten years, but every single year you enhance your ability to do your job better, more efficiently, and to a higher degree of professionalism. A growth mindset is less about career advancement and more about demonstrating that you are a flexible, adaptable, forward thinking professional.

7. Self-Starter (Highly Motivated)

Self-motivation may be one of a hiring manager's most sought after attributes in a candidate because it directly correlates to how a hiring manager will need to invest their own time and effort in managing an employee. Employees who are

GETTING A JOB AFTER COLLEGE

motivated on their own and don't require constant supervision and prompting from their manager are more likely to be low-maintenance and highly productive additions to a team.

8. Excellent Soft Skills

Beyond how your background, education, experience, and industry knowledge qualifies you for a position, hiring managers want to know if you have the right soft skills to be a good fit for their team. These are the skills that most degrees and years in an industry won't teach you, but they are what can make or break your ability to convince a hiring manager you are a worthwhile addition. Respectful, hardworking, dependable, positive, organized, confident, works well under pressure, effective communicator, and a problem solver are a few examples of highly desirable soft skills.

9. Ability to add Value to the Organization

Think about a time you've purchased a vehicle. Beyond the year, make and model, you are interested in the additional assets a car possesses which will add value to your purchase – a sunroof, a backup camera, remote keyless entry, for example. Presenting yourself to a hiring manager is like showing yourself off as a car to a potential buyer. If you can demonstrate value in yourself as a candidate, including attributes like superior knowledge, skills or job-related abilities, you have a better chance of showing a hiring manager that you can add value to a company. What is the skill or attribute you have that will make you invaluable to a hiring manager? Find that answer and then sell that in your interview and on your resume as a way of differentiating yourself from the pack of other candidates.

10. Organization

You have to show that you can work efficiently, be able to prioritize and manage your time well. It is also important that you be able to show employers how you would work as an employee, and how you go about meeting deadlines. Demonstrate to the employer that you can work independently and as a team player. Give specific examples on how you work efficiently.

11. Confidence

In the workplace, you need to strike a balance between being confident in yourself without being arrogant and trusting in your colleagues and the company you work for.

12. Sell Yourself in the Interview Highlight your skills, experience and training to the hiring manager.

Demonstrate why you are the best candidate for the position. Show how you will excel in the position by demonstrating your strengths. Stand out by showing the skills and talents you bring to the table as an employee.

13. Leadership

You may not be on the management team right away, but you need to show the potential to inspire other colleagues and teams that may work for the company. It's about assigning and delegating tasks well, leading by a good example and setting deadlines.

14. Communication

This has to do with your written and verbal communication and listening. It's about being concise, clear, and focused. It's also about being able to tailor your message for the audience, and listening to the views of other people.

15. Ability to ask for the Job

As a job seeker, it can be easy to fall into the trap of appearing as though you are begging and desperate for employment. Even if that is the case, it's better to seem eager and excited, but never desperate. The best way to end an interview is to show that you are interested in offering your skills, experience, time and energy in exchange for employment in a way that demonstrates your eagerness. Do this by closing the interview with questions such as, "I think I could do a lot for your company and that we could work well together. Have I given you all the information you need to offer me the job?" or "I'm very interested in this job; is there anything preventing you from offering it to me right now?" A direct, honest approach to illustrating you are enthusiastic is the best way to avoid appearing desperate.

90 Interview Questions And The Best Answers You Need To Know For Successful Job Interviews

Although there are as many different possible interview questions as there are interviewers, being ready for anything helps a great deal. That is why we've taken the time to prepare this list of 100 potential interview questions to help you get prepared for your interview.

1. Tell me about yourself.

This has to be the most universal question of all time. It would be rare for a job interviewer not to start with this question. It is very tricky because the question encompasses all the things about you. The secret to answering this question is focusing on information that you can use for the job you are applying for.

The interviewer does not want you to tell him about your life story. Just focus on the vital details about you and your job experiences. Give a little background on your education (citing a few awards, honors and scholarships), afterward, on your previous employments (mention your duties and responsibilities) and your current situation.

You can also add a few of your long and short term goals. But avoid mentioning any plan to change your career in a few years.

2. What do your co-workers and boss say about you?

You need to give a specific quote or paraphrase of a boss' or a co-worker's observation about you. You can say, "When I gave my resignation letter to my boss, he asked me to reconsider because he feels that I can get the job done on time and he really likes how I handle tasks diligently." Or you can say, "My co-workers often mention that they like how I'm always enthusiastic." Mentioning such statements would be as good as your boss or co-workers saying those great things about you. Again, avoid using adjectives such as "My co-workers describe me as friendly."

3. What made you leave your previous job?

No matter what your reason for leaving your previous job, never put your former employer in a bad light. Do not bad mouth your previous boss, even if you resigned because of his negative attitude. Avoid mentioning the huge salary if this was what attracted you to the job. The best way to answer this question is by telling the interviewer that you are seeking career advancement or a better job opportunity.

4. Why should you be hired?

Answer this by mentioning your qualifications. Use your resume as your guide but avoid reading it. The important thing is for the interviewer to see that you are an asset to the company. Avoid mentioning any benefits that you can get from the job, but rather focus on why the company needs you.

5. Tell me about your experience?

This is an excellent opportunity to sell yourself, but, again, you need to know the context to answer this question adequately. The interviewer is seeking a person who may contribute quickly to the project. If you don't know the projects the company is involved in, you should ask. The information you are going to get will help you answer this question.

6. Do you have any experience related to this field?

Answer with specific experience or previous tasks that you were a part of in your previous job that relates to the position or the field. If you do not have enough experience, mention job experiences that are similar to the job.

7. Are you a team player?

Yes! You are a team player. Cite examples of how you are a team player. Mention projects that you were a part of that have been successful.

8. How do you cope when working under pressure?

Answer this positively. Mention a few examples when

working under pressure. Make it seem as though working under pressure was the norm in your previous job. Avoid saying that you panic or crumble when under pressure.

9. What kind of salary do you expect?

Avoid answering with a number. Tell the interviewer that you are willing to consider what the company can offer.

10. What do you find to be most important in a job?

If there is something really important for you to have in a job, be honest and say it. Remember, a job interview is a tool to reveal the best fit for the company. Also, you should relate this question to the current applied job to make a suitable answer. In case you are not sure about the answer, you should make a general answer such as: "I like to be challenged at work and work in a collective group. I seek jobs with career growth and advancement opportuntities."

11. Tell me about your character?

Just mention two or three of your positive characteristics. Remember that the employer is trying to determine your "suitability" to the company. Identifying the values of the company will help you give a suitable answer.

12. When can our company start benefiting from hiring you?

Be realistic and answer that you can make it in 6 months or 1 year. Certainly, the selection of suitable time to the answer is very important. You must know most of the information about the position to be able to make a persuasive answer. (For example, if this is a new position, 6 months is good though!)

13. Do you think you're more experienced than this position requires?

The true idea behind this question is: "I am afraid you only apply in this job temporarily and you will surely quit whenever you find a better opportunity." Your answer must resolve this worry. An example: "Perhaps you are right; but, when I quit my job at XYZ Company, I would like to do things that I'd prefer and are satisfied with - (demonstrate the content of the interviewed job). Your benefit when you employ me will be my particular ability and experiences that I may contribute to your company when needed."

14. How are your managerial skills?

You may state your methods of setting goals and attracting others to reach those goals. Describe the skills you usually use to motivate others in a group or to flexibly deal with a changing situation. You should base your answer on the managerial style of the company to make a suitable answer. Nevertheless, if you are not sure, be flexible and depend on the specific situations.

15. What motivated you to apply for this position?

You can answer this interview question easily if you've done your homework. Your research about the company should have provided specific details about the organization's products, history, mission and philosophy, all of which can be reasons you chose to apply for the position.

The interviewer is asking why you should be considered for the job. So use your past work or educational experiences to show that you are a good fit and would be an asset to the company.

Don't mention salary, even if that happens to be the genuine reason you're applying for the job. Employers want people who are excited about the work and the company. Money shouldn't appear to be your primary motivator.

16. Tell me about your strengths.

The interviewer is giving you permission to toot your own horn, so don't be too modest. Focus on those strengths that the company would value such as communication and leadership skills. You can also talk about your ability to problem-solve, handle stress and get along well with others. Ideally, you want to provide examples that demonstrate these strengths.

17. Tell me about your weaknesses or areas of development.

The obvious answer would be to say you have no weaknesses, but your answer won't sound believable. Let's face it; most people have areas that could use some improvement.

Of course, you don't want to give the employer a weakness that's so significant as to disqualify you as a candidate. The best way to get out of this question is to use a weakness that may also be viewed as a strength.

For example, "I need to get better at delegating. Often, I try to do everything myself, and that's not always the best use of my time." Another tactic is to explain how you're working to overcome your weakness. For example, "I'm not as familiar as I should be with Photoshop software. Lately, I've been doing online tutorials to improve my technical skills." A different strategy is to mention a minor flaw, such as, "I can be too outspoken at times, but I'm working on choosing my words more carefully and being more diplomatic."

18. Are you competitive?

While some people might think it's best to answer "no" to this interview question, many companies value a competitive nature, especially if you're applying for a sales position. As long as you don't come across as ruthless or combative, a competitive spirit is an asset.

One way to answer this question is: "I can be competitive, but I'm also a team player. I've worked in groups and recognize that what we accomplished was far greater than what I could have done on my own."

19. What are the things you like doing in your spare time?

This interview question provides you with an opportunity to show your personality. You can describe your hobbies and interests. Of course, avoid mentioning any activities that could be considered controversial or immoral. Similarly, steer clear of any subjects that could cause the interviewer concern about your commitment to the job, such as your all-encompassing care of an elderly relative or your dedication to competing in marathons around the country.

20. Do you have any questions for me?

Asking questions of the employer shows your interest. It's an opportunity to find out more about the company and the individual position so you can decide if it's right for you. Be sure your questions reflect substance. Don't ask something trivial like how long your lunch break will be.

You should prepare at least six to ten insightful questions in advance based on your research of the company prior to your interview such as: What is the size of the company in terms of sales volume and number of employees? What are the company's strengths compared to its competition? What are the main responsibilities of the position?

21. Tell me what you know about this organization.

Do your homework prior to the interview. Doing the background work will help you stand out. Find out who the main players are. Have they been in the news recently? You're not expected to know every date and individual, yet you need to have a solid understanding of the company as a whole.

22. Who are our main competitors?

This shows you really understand the industry and the main players. Think of a few competitors and say how you think they compare in similarities and differences. This is a good opportunity to highlight what you think are the company's key strengths.

23. Are you applying for other jobs?

If you are serious about changing jobs, it is likely that you are applying to other positions. This can be a way of showing that you are in demand. Although you should be honest, don't go into too much detail, you don't want to spend a great deal of time on this. If asked about names of who you have spoken to, it is absolutely legitimate to say you prefer not to disclose that information at this stage.

24. Is there any sort of person you won't like to work with?

This is not an easy one as you have no idea who you would be working with. Even if you can immediately think of a long list of people you don't like to work with, you could take some time to think and say that it's a difficult question as you have always gotten along fine with your colleagues.

25. What do you see as your biggest professional disappointment/achievement so far?

If you are asked about disappointments, mention something that was beyond your control. Stay positive by showing how you accepted the situation and have no lingering negative feelings. If asked about your greatest achievement, chose an example that was important to you as well as the company. Specify what you did, how you did it and what the results were. Ideally, pick an example that relates to the positions you are applying for.

26. Is there any kind of decision you often find difficult to make?

There is no right or wrong answer here. The logic behind this type of question is that your past behavior is likely to predict what you will do in the future. What the interviewer is looking for is to understand what you find difficult.

27. What suggestion have you made that has been implemented?

Here the emphasis is on implemented. You may have had many brilliant ideas, but the interviewer wants something that has actually materialized. Be prepared to briefly describe how it went from the idea to the implementation stage.

28. Have you ever had to bend the rules in order to achieve a goal?

Beware of this type of question! Under no circumstances is it necessary to break company policy to achieve something. Resist the temptation to answer and give examples, the interviewer is trying to determine how ethical you are and if you will remain true to company policy.

29. Would you be willing to travel or relocate if necessary?

This is something you need to have very clear in your mind prior to the meeting if you think there is any chance this may come up. There is no point in saying yes just to get the job if the real answer is actually no. Be honest as this can save you from problems arising in the future.

30. Are there any work situations that irritate or satisfy you the most?

Well, the second part of the question is easy. You may answer that you are satisfied the most when you have done your job with the best results and on schedule. You should be careful, however, with the first part of the question, but keep in mind that factors beneficial to the employer may pass this question. For example, you may mention that you don't like to be late at work or co-workers who are trying to take off their job on the shoulders of their co-workers, or that you don't like long breaks, etc.

31. What are your career goals?

Employers ask this interview question because they want to see what positions you might grow into if you are hired. The company may be looking for a candidate they can groom into their next Senior VP. However, if you are only looking for a job to cover you for the next couple of years, it might not be the best match.

32. Tell me why you should be selected over other candidates.

This is one of the most frequently asked questions in job interviews that you must answer deftly. The indirect implication or purpose of this question is to evaluate your unique features.

Everyone wants to be selected for the job and desires that he should be given preference over others. To answer this question well, you need to exhibit your exceptional attributes as well as valuable set of skills. Pinpoint your strengths and try to be very precise and yet informative.

You must consider beforehand what the employer is stressing as requirements for the job. You should have a complete list of those requirements before attending the interview. Evaluate yourself to explore some qualities inside of you that are a fit for the job.

33. In which position do you see yourself in five years?

This is another standard job interview question. It can, however, be used by a smart interviewer to highlight how well or badly the candidate has prepared. Unfortunately, most people will fall for this "trick" by simply stating that they haven't really thought about it or worse, just mumbling something like being a little higher up on the pay ladder or something else that is irrelevant. Another temptation will be to show your loyalty and state that you would like to run a department or be in another position working for the new employer. While the show of loyalty may be admirable, it's unlikely to garner respect from the interviewer as it will just seem like you are sucking up! Instead of falling for these common pitfalls, answer the question in a far more general fashion: "I would like to be in a position where I can make a substantial contribution to my employer and help make decisions that will shape the company moving forward." Alternatively, you can say something else that has a similar meaning.

34. If you encounter a difficult customer, how would you deal with such person?

This question is very common for those in sales department or jobs that involve facing the customers. An interviewer basically wants to hear you say that you are willing and able to take control of the situation and to take ownership and responsibility of the solving of the customer's problem with as little fuss as possible. While it can be tempting to pull faces and tell stories of the horrible customers you have dealt with, this should be avoided as it can give a very bad impression of your attitude toward the customers, those people who pay everyone's wages!

35. Do you prefer a specific work environment?

The interviewer will ask this leading question so that he can determine whether you are a team player or otherwise. It would be safe to answer that you have worked efficiently both in team efforts or individual tasks.

36. What have you been engaged in since your last job?

If you were fired, unemployed or show any gaps during employment address those issues in a very clear, concise and compelling way with the hiring manager. Say that you have been working on improving your skills by taking professional development courses online or attending seminars or volunteering. Once again, such claims should be validated through certificates or other documentation.

37. Tell me about your experience working with your previous supervisor.

Never speak ill of your previous boss, as this will be taken as an indication that you are probably going to do the same of a new supervisor. Instead, choose to highlight the positives and downplay any negatives. A good response would be: "My supervisor was a very dedicated worker, and this made it easy for me to carry out my responsibilities."

38. What do you consider to be your best asset?

Highlight your qualities that would make you an asset to the organization. Perhaps you work well as a team member or have the ability to motivate co-workers.

39. Describe a problem you had with your past supervisor and how it was resolved.

This also sounds strongly like a tricky question. Stay positive and develop a memory lapse about any trouble with a past supervisor.

40. Have you been involved in a conflict with your co-workers? How was it resolved?

Conflict is always a part of life and is no different in the workplace. The interviewer wants to know your social problem-solving skills and if you are a combative person. Answering no to this usually encourages the interviewer to dig deeper looking for any conflict you may have had, even if minor. It is best to pick a single example and show how you skillfully solved the problem to everyone's advantage. It is best not to give too many examples lest the interviewer think you are a trouble maker.

41. How has your education and previous work prepared you for this job?

This is a question where they want concrete examples of how you would fit the role they are offering. It is also important to show behavioral examples on how your general attitude, not just your job specific skills, would be good for their business. Give them examples that showcase your skills, attitude and work ethic. If you do not have much experience, concentrate on your attitude and examples from life or study that could be modified to show applicable skills.

42. Would you consider yourself a risktaker?

How you answer this question depends on the type of company it is. If it is a start-up company or within a highly-competitive industry, they are probably looking for those more willing to take risks. If you believe the company is this type, then offer an example of a risk you've taken in business. If the company is a well-established industry leader, risktakers are not as highly valued. Of course, there is hardly any company that is looking for employees who are foolish in their risktaking behavior, so a good rule of thumb is to place yourself somewhere in the middle: You are neither too foolish nor overly cautious.

43. Do you consider yourself to be organized? How well do you manage your time?

The interviewer wants to hear about your work skills concerning time and task management, not that you have neatly separated the paperclips in your desk drawer into different trays based on size. A model answer might be: "I manage my time very well. I routinely complete tasks ahead of schedule." For example, offer the interviewer proof of your organizational skills by telling him about a major project that you organized and completed on time or mention the fact that you consistently received an outstanding grade on previous performance reviews regarding your time management. Do not reveal to the interviewer that you are habitually late or that you complete tasks at the last minute.

44. Do you consider yourself a self-starter?

The correct answer to this question is always "yes", and the ideal answer includes an example of how you are able to work with minimal supervision, keep your skills current without being told, or a time when you took it upon yourself to be more efficient, accurate or productive.

45. How do you react to criticism from supervisors that you consider unjust?

The only correct way to answer this question is to present

yourself as a person who can handle criticism without becoming angry, defensive, vengeful or arrogant without letting others intimidate or blame you when you don't deserve it. Example: "There was a time when I was deeply hurt when a supervisor pointed out a mistake I made or an area in which I needed to improve and felt somewhat defensive. However, through the years, I have learned that no one is perfect; everyone makes mistakes and needs to improve in certain areas, so I shouldn't take criticism so personally. Therefore, I have learned to take it on the chin without becoming defensive or feeling hurt. I take time to think about what was said and if I feel the criticism is warranted, I take steps to improve my performance. If I feel the criticism was unjustified, I will sit down with my supervisor and calmly discuss the issues.

46. Do you have an aversion for doing a lot of routine work?

Don't answer with, "Oh yes, I will enjoy filing eight hours a day, 40 hours a week, 50 weeks a year!" Instead, try to assure the interviewer you aren't going to go mad doing your boring job. For example, "I know this position requires a lot of routine work, but I don't expect to start at the top. I'm willing to start at the bottom and prove myself. Eventually, I will be assigned tasks that require more brain power."

47. What reference books do you use at work?

One should not answer this question with, "I don't have any reference books." A good, safe answer is to state that you use a dictionary on a regular basis and one or two other books that are relevant to your field. For example, if you are a sales person you might respond, "I keep a dictionary handy and the book that helped me succeed in sales, *How to Win Friends and Influence People.* If your work involves accounting, then mention a few accounting reference books; if your work involves computer programming, mention a few relevant books, etc.

48. Have you ever held a position that wasn't right for you?

One can answer this question with either yes or no, but answering "no" would be better. If you answer yes, you need to explain the mistake you made in exercising good judgment. A good reason is often the lure of more money.

49. Do you find it comfortable working in a large company?

The interviewer might be asking this question because your employment history shows you've always worked for smaller companies. Always answer this question in the positive: "Yes, I would be very comfortable working for a large company. I believe that working for a large company would not only provide more opportunities for advancement and growth, but would also expose me to more areas in my field."

50. Do you find it comfortable working for a startup?

The interviewer might be asking this question because your employment history shows you've always worked for larger and more established companies. Always answer this question in the positive: "Yes, I would be very comfortable working for a startup company. I believe that working for a startup company would not only provide more opportunities for advancement and growth but would also expose me to more areas in my field.

51. How long do you think you will work for us?

When answering this question, keep in mind that it costs employers a small fortune to hire you. They have to spend thousands recruiting and training you. Therefore, they don't want you to stay for just a few months or years and then quit. However, don't assume the interviewer wants your answer to be "I will be your most devoted employee until I retire forty years from now", particularly if your resume indicates you generally stay with one employer for five years before moving on.

52. Do you expect problems to occur or just react to them?

The correct answer to this question is that you try to anticipate problems rather than react to them. You should give a brief outline of a time when you caught a problem and resolved it before it did damage to the company.

53. Describe your typical day at work.

The interviewer is trying to discover (1) if you exaggerated the job duties listed on your resume and/or (2) if you have the necessary experience to do the job for them. Therefore, your answer should emphasize the duties one would perform in the job you're trying to get. If you can, re-read the job description and emphasize the job duties listed there.

54. Do you have any physical challenges that would limit your performance on this job?

Employers have to be very careful about asking this question as too much prying can violate your civil rights. Therefore, they won't ask too many questions and you don't need to offer them very much information. The best way to answer this question is to keep it short and simple: "No, I don't have any physical problems that would affect my ability to perform this job."

55. How do you maintain a balance between your career and family?

On the surface, this question appears to be illegal, but it isn't the way that it's worded. The interviewer is hoping you will reveal information about things he isn't allowed to ask, such as if you are married, single, divorced, have children, or are straight or gay. If you don't want to reveal information about your personal life, offer a simple, vague answer: "I haven't had a problem balancing my work and private life. One has never interfered with the other. I am capable of getting the work I need to get done without it interfering with my personal life." On the other hand, you might want to reveal a great deal of information if you think it will help you get the job offer.

56. What are your reasons for wanting to leave your present job?

You could state that you want a more challenging position, higher salary, or more responsibility. Don't mention personal conflicts with your present boss or bad-mouth your current employer or co-workers as this will harm your chances of being offered the job. Keep in mind that interviewers love people who are looking for more challenging positions or responsibility because it shows drive, ambition and motivation.

57. What part of your performance was criticized most by your last supervisor?

A good way to answer this question is to offer a criticism you received that is not very important or not directly related to the position you're applying for. For example, telling the interviewer that you were constantly criticized for coming to work an hour late is not a good idea. However, revealing a minor criticism and telling the interviewer what steps you took to improve yourself is a good way to answer this question. In fact, if you can state that you have already solved the problem and received a higher mark on a subsequent performance review, then say so.

58. Have you ever been fired or asked to resign?

When answering this question, keep in mind that the interviewer knows that almost everyone has been fired at least once and it is usually due to a personality conflict with the boss or coworkers. So, if you have been fired, admit it; you should, however, do so without attacking your former boss or employer, and without sounding defensive or bitter. Do not mention that you have been fired many times unless asked specifically, "How many times have you been fired?" Have a sense of humor when discussing your firings so that the interviewer doesn't get the idea you are a nut who might come back to the workplace with an assault rifle if you're fired. Tell the interviewer what you learned from being fired. If you have been fired many times, mention what steps you have taken to improve yourself. In addition, point out any past jobs you held when you got along well with your boss and coworkers or received good performance reviews or a promotion.

59. How long have you been searching for a job?

Why haven't you received a job offer? Why have you been unemployed for so long? It is always better to answer this question with "I just started looking", but this is not always possible, particularly if your resume indicates you've been unemployed for the last six months.

If you can't hide the fact that your job search has been taking a while, state you're being selective about who you will work for. Of course, stating this might prompt the interviewer to ask, "What offers have you turned down?" which could land you in hot water if you haven't actually received any job offers. (It isn't a good idea to lie in answering this latter question.) A bad economy and a crowded market are good reasons one might have trouble finding a job.

However, be aware that many interviewers will hold this against you even if the job market was very bad and many people were having trouble finding employment.

60. Out of your previous jobs, which one do you consider to be your favorite and why?

This is actually a trick question asked to determine if you enjoy the type of work the position you're applying for involves. Therefore, the answer to this question should be a job that requires the same or similar work that you will be required to perform in the new job. If you do not have a previous job wherein you performed similar tasks, offer an answer that does not suggest you are ill-suited for the position. For example, if you are applying for a high-stress, demanding job in a chaotic environment, don't tell the interviewer you loved your position with company A because of the mellow, low stress "work at your own pace" atmosphere.

61. Would you choose the same career if you could start over again?

How you answer this question depends on whether or not you are trying to win a job related to your career history or are trying to enter a new field. No matter how much you despise the career you originally chose, do not admit this fact to the interviewer because it tells him you consider your work to be drudge. If you are trying to enter a new field, of course, tell the interviewer that you would choose the field you're now trying to enter if you had it to do all over again; that's why you're trying to enter it now.

62. Why have you been working with the same employer for so long?

Just as moving from job to job too frequently can harm you, so can staying with the same employer for too long, particularly if you've never been promoted and your resume indicates you haven't been intellectually challenged in years. Your answer should state something about your having worked successfully with many people both inside and outside of the organization, including different bosses and co-workers, as well as interacting regularly with various types of organizations and customers.

63. What has made you change jobs so frequently?

Reasons for job-hopping should be based on your past employers' failure to challenge you, failure to give you enough opportunity for advancement, because you needed more money, or for family reasons, and never on the fact that your past employers were incompetent, dumb, or unfair. Do not indicate in any way that you are hard to get along with or get bored and leave at the drop of a hat, and make sure you point out any jobs you did hold for a long time. Mention that your current goal is long-term employment and back that up with any proof you have to want job stability such as a new baby, new marriage, new home, etc. If the job you're applying for offers you the challenges and environment you were always looking for, make sure you point out this fact.

64. What could you have done to improve your relationship with your least favorite boss?

Again, refrain from stating negativities about your former boss. Put a positive spin on your answer by telling the interviewer that if you had it to do all over again, you would have requested more feedback from your boss regarding your performance and requested to be assigned more projects, etc.

65. Have any of your past employers refused to give you a reference?

Of course, the best answer to this question is "no", but if you have to answer "yes", explain why in a professional manner. In other words, don't complain bitterly about the employer who refused to give you a reference. Sample answer: "Yes, John Wilson at company A refused to give me a reference because he is unhappy that I resigned from the company. This is unfortunate because John and I really liked each other and worked well together. I did receive excellent performance reviews and two raises based on performance while at company A, so his refusal to give me a reference is not based on poor performance. As I said, he is angry at me for resigning because he considers my doing so to be disloyal to the company."

66. What are the reasons for the gaps in your employment history?

Answer this question by explaining each gap in your work history that is longer than six months. You should try to put a positive spin on your answer. Good reasons to explain away employment gaps are that you took some time off to raise your children or to go back to school and get your degree or obtain necessary training to get a better job. Although not ideal, acceptable reasons to explain employment gaps are that you took a year off to travel or that the economy has been very bad and you simply couldn't find work in a year and a half. Don't say it was because "no one would hire me" or "I kept getting fired" without putting a positive spin on your answer. Mention that your current goal is long-term employment and back that up with any proof you have to want job stability such as a new baby, new marriage, new home, etc. If the job you're applying for offers you the challenges and environment you were always looking for, you should point out that fact.

67. Would your present employer be surprised to know you're job hunting?

Never answer this question with negative information such as "My current boss wouldn't be surprised, in the least, to hear that I'm leaving since he's been trying to shove me out the door for years!" Always tell the interviewer that you are happy with your current employer and job, but are simply looking to stretch your wings out and take on a job with more challenge, and yes, more salary and opportunities for advancement.

68. What would you do if a supervisor asked you to do something the wrong way?

The interviewer is testing how insubordinate you might

be. Never answer this question by claiming you would refuse to do something the way the supervisor told you to do it unless you are required by your company or by law to follow certain procedures. Instead, tell the interviewer you would tell the supervisor you think it should be done another way. Nevertheless, if the supervisor insisted you do it his way, you would do so.

69. What kind of people do you have trouble getting along with?

You don't want to answer this question with "Hard-working people who make lazy people like me look bad." You want to be the hard-working, nice person who doesn't like lazy or difficult people. However, be careful; the position you're interviewing for might come with an unpleasant, difficult supervisor and the interviewer is asking you this question for that reason.

"I don't get along well with people who don't hold up their end of the job, who are constantly coming in late or calling in sick. They don't really respect their co-workers and bring the whole organization down."

70. Why do you want to work for this company?

Don't answer this question with, "Because you advertised for an X at abcabc.com." Your answer should offer what you think are the most interesting aspects of the company, for example, "because it is on the cutting edge of technology" or "because you are the industry leader". The research you do on the company to prepare for the interview should give you an answer to this question.

71. When can you start working with this company?

It is customary for most employees to give at least two weeks' notice to their current employer. Those in management positions are expected to give longer notice. You will not earn points if you express disrespect toward your current employer by telling the interviewer that you plan to quit your present job without giving sufficient notice. He will assume you will show his company the same amount of disrespect. It is also a good idea to tell the interviewer you plan to start learning about your new position/employer on your off-hours (i.e., reading employee training manuals, etc.) Telling the interviewer you can't begin work for a few months because you want to take some time off is not a good idea.

72. What is your commitment to this job?

Most people would respond with an answer avowing a deep commitment to the company and the job; however, a better answer would be to state that your commitment would grow as you get to know the company and the people in it.

73. Aren't you overqualified for this job?

Note that employers don't like to hire overqualified people because they won't stay around long. But if it is obvious that you're overqualified, admit that you are, but also emphasize the positive. For example: "I am overqualified in some ways.

I have more experience than required for this job, but you are looking for someone who is an expert in X, and that's me. However, that doesn't mean I'm completely overqualified. I feel that I have much to learn in the area of X, which is a big part of this job and I know it will keep me challenged."

74. Why should we pay you the salary you're requesting?

Answer this question by convincing the interviewer that you deserve the salary you're requesting. The best way to do this is to point out how you have benefited your past employers in terms of increasing profit, reducing expenses, improving efficiency, etc.

75. Would you like to tell me anything else about yourself?

This question is usually one of the last asked. Don't answer with a simple "No." Instead, use this question to try to get the job offer. You can do this by answering, "Yes, you should know that I really want this job. After talking with you today, I feel that this is a position that would provide me with lots of opportunities to grow and stretch my wings and I feel I could really contribute to this company. I have the sales experience and ability you're looking for and the required supervisory skills as well. Is there anything that prevents you from offering me this position today?

76. Tell me what you have heard about our company that you don't like.

There is probably a need for you to do research to answer

this question, particularly if the company isn't well known and you haven't heard anything about the company. If you don't know of anything negative, then answer, "I honestly haven't heard anything negative about your company. I did some research on your company before answering your classified ad and I didn't come across anything negative." If you have heard some bad news about the company, such as the fact that it is unstable or operating in the red, then say so: "I have heard that last year's profits were way down and I am concerned about this."

77. *What aspect of this job appeals to you the least?*

In asking this question, the interviewer is trying to determine if you dislike doing a major part of your job. For example, if you're a file clerk, you obviously don't want to answer by stating that you hate to file. Like most people, you probably hate doing the routine, boring administrative tasks that everyone has to do; therefore, you might want to answer accordingly: "I don't particularly like compiling the monthly sales reports. I love the sales process, meeting and negotiating with clients, working out in the field all day. Sitting in front of a computer for a few hours each month doesn't particularly appeal to me. I know it needs to be done, and I've always done this task as required in my previous jobs, but I don't particularly like doing it."

78. *How will you handle the parts of this job you like the least?*

This question is very similar to the question before this

and should be answered positively: "I will perform all of the tasks my job requires on time and to the best of my ability regardless of whether or not I enjoy them."

79. Do you know who our major competitors are?

You do not want to answer "No" this question. In fact, being able to discuss who their competitors are in-depth can only help you get the job. You need to research this question before the interview and know who their top competitors are. A good answer: "Yes, your three major competitors are A, B, and C. Currently, you are the industry leader. However, B has plans to enter the X sector and challenge your dominance in this market." You might want to learn about each company's strengths and weaknesses as well.

80. What was the reason behind your decision to attend X College? Are you happy with your choice?

Always state that you are happy with your choice, even if you aren't. Do not state, "It was the only place that would accept me." Do not make negative statements about the school or your professors either. A good reason for choosing a particular school is that you liked the particular program they offered or it is known for offering a good education in your particular major.

81. What were the factors you considered when choosing your major?

A great answer is to state that you have always wanted

to become X since you were a child and selected your major accordingly. If you're changing career fields or applying for a position unrelated to your major, tell the interviewer you were interested in that subject at the time, but circumstances haven't taken you down a new path. Of course, you should also put a positive spin on it by stating that you have benefited tremendously from changing careers (learned new things, made you more hardworking, etc.).

82. What is your GPA? Do you feel it reflects your true abilities?

If your GPA is high, then this question is easy: "My GPA is 3.8." If your GPA is not that good, perhaps you can make it better by calculating your GPA for only coursework related to your major. Example: "My overall GPA is not that good, 2.8; however, if you consider only my engineering coursework, my GPA is 3.8. It was the required coursework I had to take in English and political science that dragged my GPA down. And no, it isn't an accurate reflection of my abilities. I had to work part-time to support myself while attending the university. I had a limited amount of study time, and I thought it best to spend it on engineering subjects rather than political science and English."

83. How has your schooling (internships) prepared you for this position?

Don't tell the interviewer that your schooling or internship has completely prepared you for the position, because it did not. Sample answer: "My internships have prepared me for this position by giving me basic real-world experience in the accounting field. The most important lesson my internships taught me is that the accounting skills I learned from college textbooks is not enough. The real world presents you with problems and situations not found in a textbook. My internships allowed me to significantly improve my skills in the areas of preparing monthly statements, handling accounts receivable and payable, and completing tax returns for small businesses and so I feel I'm a good candidate for this position as these tasks are a major part of this job."

84. If you were given an opportunity for a do over, would you choose the same major?

Always say that you would choose the same major even if you wouldn't. If you don't, the interviewer might think you don't really know who you are or what you want, and consequently, might not be a very good worker or stay with the company very long. Good answer: "Yes, I would definitely choose the same major since I am very interested in computer science."

85. What was your favorite course in college and why?

Always answer this question with a serious course related to your major. Good answer: "I particularly enjoyed statistics, which might seem strange, since most people detest it. I think I liked it so much because I was particularly good at it. In fact, the professor asked me to be a tutor to other students having difficulty with the material."

86. How did your college experience change you?

Obviously, your college experience prepared you to enter the workforce, but what else does the interviewer want to hear? You emerged from your college experience well rounded, introspective, hard-working, disciplined, mature, etc. Good answer: "When I entered the university four years ago I thought I knew what to expect in college and what it meant to be a teacher. But two years into college, I began to appreciate the hard work and dedication required to be a good teacher. I think my college experience changed me in that I have greater respect for teachers and the education industry than I did when I first entered college."

87. Do you intend to further your education?

Almost every job requires learning and improving. Therefore, you don't want to give the impression that you don't like learning or improving by saying, "No, I'm through with school. I never want to sit in a classroom again!" Instead, it would be better if you claim you will be earning a degree, graduate degree, taking continuing education classes, etc., even if you aren't that committed to further education.

88. Why were your grades not very good in school?

There are several legitimate and believable answers to this question. One might be that you had to work full-time in order to support yourself. Another might be that you just aren't very good at taking tests. In any event, if your grades were not that good, you're going to have to say something to overcome it. Don't blame it on others, such as your professors, who "were out to get you." Take responsibility for it: "I know my grades weren't that good in school, but I've never been very good at taking tests. I don't think my grades are an accurate reflection of my ability. I feel that I know this field as well as any new graduate. I just don't do well on tests."

89. Why are you applying for a job unrelated to your internship experiences?

A good answer to this question is to state that your internship opportunities were not related to the career path you wanted to concentrate on and you took the internship just to get some experience in the field or that you learned from your internship experience that you like a particular area of your chosen field. Example: "There were a limited number of internships and I did not have the luxury of picking and choosing from many internships that matched my areas of interest. I thought it was better for me to get some experience in the field, even if it was in an area of accounting that didn't particularly interest me."

90. Why are you applying for a job not related to your degree?

This is a tricky question, do not answer by saying, "I decided after graduation that I didn't like my degree choice and want work in another field." If you can't find a job in your chosen field and are interviewing for other jobs, then just say something along these lines: "As I'm sure you know, thousands of computer-related jobs have been outsourced to other countries, and many of us have been left unemployed and unable to find work in the field. Therefore, I'm concentrating on finding a position that utilizes my accounting skills." Of course, if you are a liberal arts graduate, chances are high you won't find a job that requires a degree in history, political science, English, etc., and so you have a good excuse: "I majored in history because I love the subject; however, there are few jobs that require a history degree. Like most liberal arts majors, I would probably have to earn a master's or doctorate in history and get a teaching certificate in order to fully utilize my degree. I don't know if I will ever go back to school and earn an advanced degree, but in the meantime, I need to work and support myself and have chosen this field as one in which I would enjoy working."

You should endeavor to tailor your answers to the specific industry you are interviewing within. Use the questions as a guide to prepare yourself. Remember to comport yourself while answering the questions as some of them are obvious behavioral questions.

CHAPTER 9

10 Keys To A Successful Telephone Job Interview

These days, some interviewers invite candidates to do telephone interviews to select the right candidate for the job. The first impression you make is important when it comes to a telephone interview. The speech confidence you display might be the only thing you need to be successful.

While job hunting, you should be ready for any calls and be polite when answering them. When you receive an interview call, you should sell your skills, qualifications and your strengths in a convincing manner to the interviewer.

The following are ten keys to having a successful telephone interview:

1. Have control over your environment.

It is important you be in a place that is free of distractions and noise. Give your interviewer your full attention and, by all means, ensure your phone has stable reception. You may be presented with the opportunity of choosing a date and time convenient for your interview. If that arises, make the best choice for yourself.

2. Prepare adequately.

Like a physical interview, make sure that you are well prepared. Research the company and become familiar with the job description prior to the interview date. Having most of the necessary information will give you confidence in responding to questions asked by the interviewer. Keep your resume handy as you may be giving a brief explanation on some of its contents.

3. Voice training and a relaxed composure.

Perfect your grammar and tense agreement prior to your interview date. Avoid using ambiguous words and be clear in your speech. Be calm and relaxed speaking to avoid stuttering. Also, smile while answering your calls, since people can hear you smile. You could also do some practice with your friend to evaluate your level of preparedness before the main day.

4. Prepare your questions.

Most interviewers give candidates the opportunity to ask questions after the interview. Do not use this opportunity to ask about salary or benefits, start dates or what the company will do for you if employed, asking those questions will give the impression that you are more interested in the salary and benefits than the job. You could use this opportunity to show your enthusiasm and zeal, if given a chance to work.

5. Send a thank you message.

Show an act of gratitude by sending a thank you message. This goes a long way to demonstrate that you appreciate the time spent with you. A short email of thanks will be perfect. Try not to make the message generic.

6. Keep writing materials handy.

Always keep a pen and paper handy, you may receive an impromptu telephone interview and will have to take down some notes.

7. Turn of call-waiting on your phone.

Call waiting can be a huge distraction during interview calls as it can interrupt or sometimes disconnect your call. During the period of your job hunting, you would do well to turn off call waiting on your phone so that you will only have one caller to respond to at a time.

8. Keep your resume handy.

Your resume should be kept in clear view. You can tape it to the wall near the phone or on top of your desk. Doing this will make it easy for you to scan through your resume when you want to answer questions.

9. Have a list of your accomplishments available.

Just like your resume, you should have a list of your

achievements handy because the interviewer may ask questions about your accomplishments.

10. Use a landline, if possible.

If you own a landline, use it instead of your cell phone. Doing this will eliminate the possibility of a dropped call due to poor reception as landlines are known for stronger signal reception.

10 Things Interviewers And Hiring Managers Look For In Job Candidates (Top Soft Skills)

In a job interview, you have the chance to accomplish one of your dreams of getting the job that you want. By preparing for the interview, you are getting as close to this accomplishment as you can. It is important to be able to think as an employer so that you can say what your interviewer wants to hear, what he wants to be done, and act the way he (or she) likes.

When you are interviewing for a competitive job opening, you need to know how to make yourself stand out during the interview process. There are a few soft skills you can use to stand out and impress a hiring manager.

Soft skills can be defined as the set of communication habits, personality traits, charm and positive behaviors that come into play when an individual interacts with another person. One might fall into the trap of thinking that soft skills can only be applicable in jobs such as sales where person to person interaction is key, but this is not true. If an IT technician in a company is able to effectively communicate with other business units within a company, productivity within that company would increase significantly and that particular technician would be viewed in higher regard.

Training courses for such skills are increasingly being offered to aid individuals to improve themselves and allow them to be better at their jobs. Examples of such training courses would be Power Speaking, Implementing Change, and Memory Empowerment to name a few. And while these may just be a few of the popular examples of soft skills, various others also qualify: being flexible, adaptability to change, creative thinking and tolerance to cultural diversity. There are some soft skills you may innately possess.

Of course soft skills are, by no means, the sole deciding factor that employers base their hiring process on but they go a long way toward impressing a hiring manager.

So what crucial soft skills, those under-taught skills that will make the difference between getting and keeping that job, do you need?

1. Time management

This has far more to do with managing yourself rather than time. If success depends on effective action, then that action is your ability to focus your attention where it's needed most and not responding solely on how you feel at the moment. This is going to be challenging. You have multiple demands and many distractions. And you're going to be used to shifting your focus – you do it all the time flitting between Facebook, a work project, a text message and surfing the web in a matter of minutes. Being "busy" doesn't equal being productive and effective!

2. Communication

Think about how you come across to others. Empathy is a key skill you need to actively nurture both on and off-line. Your presentation skills must be meticulous for any interview – that's a threshold requirement. You need confidence to project yourself, speak honestly about your strengths and weaknesses and communicate with passion and integrity.

Good communication skills are in big demand in any career, yet employers often cite these skills as lacking in the workplace. This is a little surprising since most of us communicate with other people on a daily basis.

We communicate with different people in different ways and knowing the appropriate forms of communication in a work environment matters when it comes to finding a job.

Young people use abbreviations when texting or emailing each other, which is fine, but can become a problem if they don't know how to spell and construct sentences properly as well as understand text-speak.

If you are good at spelling and have a decent grasp of basic grammar, you are at an advantage in the job market. If you can't spell and haven't got a clue about grammar, don't despair - it's not difficult to learn. Everything you need is free online, just do a simple Google search. As an alternative, if you prefer to use a book, there are plenty of resources you can find at your local library. Fifteen to twenty minutes a day should soon get your written communication up to scratch.

3. Networking

How good are you at this skill? We live in a world dominated by constant information exchanges and daily innovation. Your relationships are your only competitive advantage and they create the channel through which ideas and information flow, where new ideas are shared, discussed and perfected. If you can cultivate a large relationship network you will meet the right people, find that job, build a business, learn about new trends, and spread ideas.

4. Writing

This is a lost skill and one that might not have been taught properly in the first place. Shocking but true. You absolutely have to be able to write proficiently so that others can understand you. Writing well goes for everything from your emails to cover letters to your CV. Write clearly, directly and intelligently. Use your writing skills to take useful notes - one of the most productive things you can do because they'll help you remember what you see, hear or read when you're learning something new or trying to remember something specific.

5. Optimism

You may think that how you act is a product of how you

are feeling, but actually you will find that you can change the way you are feeling by how you act. A great attitude always leads to great experiences. And you're going to need that great attitude no matter what life throws at you. You've got to be able to generate and radiate goodwill to maintain a competitive edge. Optimism can be learned.

6. Critical Thinking

Every day you're bombarded with vast amounts of rapidly changing information. You need to be able to evaluate it, sort the valuable from the trivial, analyze its relevance and meaning and relate it to other information, and you need to be able to do this fast. This is raw material for success today! Without this ability and awareness of thinking sharply, you'll be left behind. You've got to be able to challenge assumptions, look at things from lots of different angles, think outside the box, collaborate with others and be solution-focused.

7. Personality

This depends on the job you are applying for. You might be required to be a team player to fit in a group that is already working, or you might be required to have leadership and management skills if you are going to supervise that group. Whatever the personality required for the job you'll need to send a message, both with words and your behavior, to your interviewer that you have those skills.

8. Adaptability

Being able to adapt to changing circumstances, emergencies and any of the other unpredictable events that occur in the workplace is a critical skill in the current climate.

These soft skills are all also transferable skills, and so there is a strong likelihood that you will be able to draw upon many of your life experiences if you have not used them in the workplace. Be sure to show these skills, it will boost your chances of getting the job after the interview.

9. People Skills

This covers quite a range and includes the ability to get on with people from all walks of life and to work in a team and to take instructions from your supervisors. Interpersonal skills are gained in just about every part of life from school and college to work and social occasions. So these are truly transferable skills and even if you don't have much work experience, you should have plenty of examples to call upon.

10. Creativity and Problem-solving Skills

Employers highly value the ability to apply both logic and creativity to solve problems. If you are the kind of person who tries to see the solution as well as the problem, this will stand you in good stead.

Examples of Soft Skill Questions

After my first couple of months here, I was assigned (whatever). I had never done this before and felt I didn't have the experience to do a good job at (and on and on and on). Have you ever been in a similar situation? (Really asking: Are you the can-do- type?)

I don't usually bend the rules to get a job done. Have you ever broken the rules? (Trick question: Can you think outside the box to solve a problem?)

I'm an introvert/extrovert. Do you work better alone or in a group? (Are you capable of teamwork?)

Our department is expected to meet deadlines. If your deadline was in 1 hour and a co-worker was having problems with the copier, what would you do? (Really asking would you spend a couple of minutes and help your co-worker?)

Sometimes our department does not get complete information from our corporate office. Has anything ever gone wrong because you didn't get all the information? (Really asking: Was your verbal/written communication skill the problem?). The most frequently used communication ability question is "Do you have any questions for me?"

Ways to Build Soft Skills

Employers want recent examples of your interpersonal skills. They don't usually care what you did more than 1 or 2 years ago. This can be a challenge for new graduates and people who have been out of the workforce for an extended period. Luckily, there are many ways you can keep your talents up-to-date.

Learning something new demonstrates your can-do attitude and problem-solving skills. Scanning the job postings for "preferred" items can be your source of inspiration. You want a job, but you don't have certain requirements. First, you are proactive in learning the skills that the employer wants. Second, you have solved the problem of joblessness.

Volunteering is a noble way of building teamwork and service skills. Most nonprofit community service agencies have seen declining donations due to economic conditions. There is still much for them to do, but little funding to implement their plans. Many organizations more than welcome volunteer expertise to help organize programs, contact donors and assist with office work.

Starting a support group or action committee showcases creative problem solving, teamwork, and service talents. Start in your neighborhood. Do elderly neighbors need transportation for errands? Are children tripping on uneven sidewalks lining many of the streets? Identify a problem, form a group, find a solution, and solve the problem with results.

Writing is an excellent way to exercise your capacity for written communication. Start a blog or write for an online magazine in your area of expertise. The employer would have an easily accessible example of your written communication style.

10 Ways To Leave A Lasting Impression With Interviewers And Hiring Managers

You recently landed an interview for an incredible entry level position you discovered online or through your network. Now, the question is, how do you leave a lasting impression with hiring managers and interviewers? It can be a huge relief to receive the interview call for this position. Your foot is now halfway in the officially open door. Now it's time to walk past the door and make a great impression. How do you deliver a solid strong interview? Incorporate these ten important points when getting ready for your next interview to make a lasting impression that will land you the job:

1. Be likeable.

Employers hire people they like, so be your genuine self and be likable. You will not get the job if the hiring manager feels they can't work with you on a daily basis. This is regardless of how qualified for the job you are. You can lose an opportunity you're perfectly qualified for to an averagely qualified person, owing to the simple reason that there was a strong rapport between the hiring manager and the moderately qualified person.

2. Don't try so hard.

This doesn't mean that you shouldn't be serious, or that you should be aloof about the job. No, it means you should simply relax and be who you are without trying hard to be who they want. You don't want to be a fit with your prospective organization as the person you're trying to be, but as the person you are. What we are saying here is that even though it is important to project yourself as the person the organization wants, you should be able to do it without necessarily faking your identity.

3. See that the job fits what you want and who you are.

Don't try to change yourself to fit in with the organization. What makes a perfect employment match is an employee taking responsibility for making sure the role is a good fit for them, in addition to the company ensuring the employee is good for their organization. Some hiring decisions do not work because employees take jobs only to discover later that it's not what they want.

4. Discover the employer's problems and outline how you can solve them.

You can always get to know the challenges the organization

is facing through your interview research. Use your knowledge to devise a means of solving these problems and proffer solutions to eliminate or reduce the issues. In this way, you show the company how they will be benefiting from hiring you.

5. Show that you can apply your company research.

In doing company research, your goal shouldn't just be to be look up some basic company information on Google. Nobody will assess you based on that. What they want to see is how you use that research. Know what the company is into. Outline how you may make improvements when asked. You can show a better knowledge of the company's finances by proffering solutions on how money can be spent more wisely. Likewise, know about the company's competitors. The key is to show that you can use deductive reasoning to make a difference in performance with the information you researched.

6. Talk about information you've already mentioned in your cover letter and resume.

Recruiters go through a whole lot of resumes every day. So, just because they have read your resume before doesn't mean that they remember everything that is in it. Verbally discussing the points on your resume helps put a face to your name making you memorable.

7. Be specific.

Almost every employer has heard the line "I am a team player." But what they haven't heard is how you supervised a team that developed a project in your final year in college. These details make you stand out from the rest of the pack. Be ready to tell the story surrounding your challenges and achievements.

8. Stay positive.

If you hate your current unemployment status, it's totally your personal business and not what anybody wants to hear. Why you are the best fit for the job is all they want to hear. Connect the dots during the interview for the hiring manager. Build a rapport with the hiring manager and show them how you are excited about the position and will be a good fit within the organization.

9. Follow-up.

Follow-up, in this sense, doesn't just mean sending a generic thank you message. It goes beyond that. You can send a handwritten note via express mail to the hiring manager. While doing this, try to reference specific points from your interview as that will separate you from the crowd.

10. Allot more than the right amount of time on your schedule.

By every means possible, try to clear your schedule around the period of the interview as it will help you clear your head and keep you focused. There's no guarantee that an interview will last thirty minutes or sixty and if you're worried you might be late to your next appointment, the distraction will be evident.

Leaving a lasting impression with hiring managers during an interview isn't something that just comes from playing guessing games. It is a product of research and being prepared as best you can. Follow these tactics, in addition to the other tips in this book, and pretty soon you will be opening that door each day headed to your new job.

CHAPTER 12

How To Turn A Job Interview Into A Job Offer - 7 Steps To Make A Connection And Get Hired

How do you make a lasting, memorable connection with another person? You empathize with them. You work to uncover their pain (which is to say, a problem they are currently experiencing), understand that pain, and propose a solution for it. You create a relationship where you are adding real value to the other person's life.

What does this have to do with job interviews? You'd be surprised: Growing evidence suggests that making a memorable connection with a hiring manager—and the business they represent—is a critical step during the interview process.

All too often, we leave our natural interpersonal skills and instincts at the door when we enter job interviews, assuming that professional interactions require a detached attitude. However, while it's true that professional conversations should be focused and structured, the principles that drive engagement are fairly universal. The key to turning a job interview into a job offer lies in making an emotional connection with the hiring manager, one that allows you to identify the business's "pain" (a problem the company urgently needs to address).

Step One: Understanding the Difference between Assets and Value

The majority of job candidates make the same mistake: They think that the hiring manager's top priority is to answer the question, "Why should we hire you?" To be more precise, they believe that the hiring manager wants to review the skills and experience (the assets) of each candidate. They think that the hiring manager's primary aim is to choose the candidate with the most experience and the greatest number of relevant skills. They assume that the purpose of an interview is to verify the authenticity of the job candidate's claims and make sure they have an appropriately professional demeanor.

The hiring manager is, therefore, looking for what sets you apart from many of the other similarly-qualified candidates—in other words, your value. Discovering this hinges on answering a different question altogether: "What problem would hiring you solve?"

While you can learn a lot about a person's history and skill level by reading through their resume, what you can't usually figure out "on paper" is how they think. After all, resumes and cover letters are often rewritten multiple times, sometimes with the aid of senior professionals and professional writers and editors. When a hiring manager brings you into a more dynamic, real-time environment—the interview—what they really want to do is test your problem-solving skills.

In an ideal world, your interviewer would have some excellent value-probing questions written and rehearsed, making this process clear-cut. But of course, we're not living in an ideal world, and more often than not the job candidate has to guide the value-sharing process. This is where having an established and practiced interview technique becomes vital: Interviewers often don't have a lot of time (and consequently patience) for the interview process. Interviewing you is taking precious minutes away from their usual duties and costing the company money.

They want to know whether or not you can do the job well, and they want to know ASAP.

At the same time, however, hiring managers have been known to ask vague or off-beat questions that seem to have little to do with the offered position, e.g., "Imagine yourself as an animal. What animal would you be, and why?" When this happens, if you haven't prepared yourself adequately, it's easy to get thrown off balance. Tricky questions like these can cause you to misread the interviewer's needs and throw your focus off discovering the business's pain, resulting in a less memorable interview.

To prevent the above from happening, you need to rehearse for your interviews in the correct way. Through using the interview advice presented herein, you are going to learn how to keep your eye on the prize.

Step Two: Understanding Business Pain

To discover a company's "business pain," you'll first need to have a complete and specific understanding of what business pain is, exactly. Ask probing questions that focus on uncovering the problems with the hiring manager or interviewers department. The goal of uncovering the hiring managers "business pain" is to make an emotional connection, by showing your problem-solving skills and stand out as a must "hire."

Step Three: Finding Business Pain with Probing Questions

Here are some questions to ask the hiring manager or interviewer and start engaging them:

1. What are some of the problems your department faces right now?
2. What problems need to be addressed in the next 30, 60 or 90 days?
3. What are some of the challenges in this position?
4. What do you want the employee to accomplish in this position in the first 90 days?
5. Can you tell me about the team I will be working with?
6. How would you describe the responsibilities of this position?
7. How would you describe a typical day in this position?
8. How would you describe your management style?
9. What is the key to success in this position?
10. How is success measured in this position by you?

Step Four: Selling Your Problem Solving Skills

Spontaneously demonstrating problem solving abilities is a major stumbling block for many interview candidates. It's easy to create uncomfortable pauses while you stop to think, for example, or you may express your ideas in a vague or confusing manner without realizing it. Fortunately, there's a way to prepare for this stage of the interview as well: The STAR formula.

The STAR (Situation, Tasks, Action, and Results) formula provides a model for shaping your existing experiences into specific examples of when you solved problems similar to the ones the business is experiencing. The STAR formula can be broken down as follows:

1. *Situation:* Think of a challenging situation you've encountered that you believe is similar to the business's current pain. If you have never dealt with the exact issue, the business is having before, either pick the closest available equivalent or look for a situation you experienced where you developed highly transferable skills.

2. *Task:* What did you have to achieve to resolve the challenging situation, e.g. what task were you given and how did you complete it successfully despite the obstacles in your way? If you were not assigned a specific task and instead devised your own course of action, you may wish to think of the T in STAR as "Target" rather than "Task." Your Target is the goal you set for yourself to resolve the challenging situation. Talk about how you came to the

conclusion this goal was the right one and then describe how you achieved it.

3. *Action:* As you talk about how you carried out your Task or achieved your Target goal, don't forget to describe the specific actions you took. Vague examples like "I improved our marketing efforts" will not convey your real value; always talk about how you did things rather than just stating what you did.

4. *Results:* Describe the outcome of your actions to the hiring manager. Once again, be as specific as possible, using hard data like facts and figures wherever possible (for instance, "I increased social media engagement by 30%, which drove a subsequent 15% increase in sales during the fourth quarter of 2015"). You should follow up by mentioning what you learned as a result of your experience and how you've implemented the skills you gained since.

If the STAR formula does not work for your experience (it may not fit if, for example, you're talking about an experience you had as the owner of a small business), you can choose the simpler PAR formula. The PAR formula is more straightforward, requiring that you describe a Problem; afterward, discuss your Actions and Results in the manner described above.

Step Five: Building Emotional Trust as the "Must Hire."

As useful as the STAR formula is, by itself, it will not guarantee that you gain the most important thing of all: The hiring manager's trust. If, for example, you try too hard to portray yourself as the one and only candidate who can magically solve all of the business's woes—the candidate who has "all of the answers"—your use of the STAR formula may well backfire. Candidates who do this come across as arrogant and even condescending, not to mention the fact that hiring managers are not naive: They have probably interviewed dozens of candidates during their careers. By now, they know that candidates who seem too good to be true are probably less than genuine. And the moment you lose your credibility in this way, you've lost your shot at the job.

Step Six: Asking For the Job

A surprising number of candidates, once they realize their interview has gone well, feel such a wave of relief that they forget to cross the official finish line: They fail to ask for the job. This is a grave error because, if you do this, you risk looking less driven and less serious about the position than other candidates who directly ask for the job. Remember: It's not enough to be able to do the job; your hiring manager needs to know you want to do the job. They want to feel like your interview with them is not "just another interview" to you.

There is, of course, a certain finesse to asking for the job. If you look desperate, the hiring manager will immediately wonder why, and doubt will creep into the trust you just worked so hard to establish with them. Rather than coming right out and saying something like, "So, do I have the job?" or, "May I please have the job?" Try looking the hiring manager in the eye while telling them that you'd love to work for their company. Follow your statement up with three or four concise reasons why you feel this way. You might, for example, cite your belief in the quality of the company's products or talk about your admiration for a key player's contributions to your industry. Whichever quality you choose to highlight, be as specific as possible when you mention why you feel the way you do. If you come across like you're flattering the company solely for the sake of getting the job, your credibility will suffer.

Step Seven: Sending a Thank You Letter

A thank you letter is much more than just a polite formality—it's your final opportunity to emphasize your value before the interview process is officially over. For this reason, you should never, ever send a cursory generic thank you letter.

A lot of information tends to get "lost" during and after verbal conversations. The hiring manager might have become distracted when you were delivering a key point, for example. Or perhaps, right after the interview ended, there was a workplace crisis she had to attend to. Maybe she was especially tired that day after having interviewed some candidates in succession (this is typically the case with afternoon interviews). Your thank you letter is your one chance to mitigate these risks and reiterate your value, so make it count.

This is not to suggest, of course, that you should write a three-page transcript covering the entire interview—no one will have time to read such a missive. Instead, choose three or four highlights that will affirm your position as an excellent and qualified problem solver. List these as bullet points while making sure that each point clearly conveys a benefit you will add to the company (be sure to relate these benefits to solving the business pain). Like your resume, cover letter, and interview, your thank you letter should answer the ultimate question: "What problem would hiring you solve?" Keep your focus on the company—what's in it for the organization and the hiring manager—rather than describing your skills and competencies for the sake of making yourself look supremely qualified.

25 Brilliant Questions to Ask Interviewers or Hiring Managers

As you've seen in one of the steps outlined above, it is important that you engage your interviewer with brilliant questions. This is why we have compiled 25 questions you can ask the interviewer to keep them engaged.

1. Have I answered all your questions?

This question gives you the chance to touch all important aspects of your strengths which you may not have covered during the interview. It will also help to remove any doubt the interviewers may have about your competence and suitability for the job.

2. What does a normal workday look like?

This will allow you to know the number of hours you'll be spending on the job if you eventually get it. It also shows the interviewer how eager you are to start the job.

3. What do you enjoy about working here?

This question can help you establish an emotional connection with your interviewer which will differentiate you from other applicants. It will also let you know what the working condition of the organization is like.

4. How much are you willing to pay for the position?

At a final interview, you can be firm and go into specifics about the financial remuneration of the position you applied for. You can be firm regarding the salary that you want for the talent, skills, training and experience you will bring to the organization.

5. Why is this opening available?

If a lot of people have shuffled through the position you are applying for in three years, it speaks volumes about the kind of organization you are about to be a part of. But if it's a position that is newly created, it goes to show that the company is growing.

6. Who are the people I'd be working with?

Asking this question leaves you with information regarding the organization's staff, strengths and turnovers. A simple question like "How many new persons have you hired in the last year?" can give you the necessary information you need regarding the organization's turnover rate.

7. Are there opportunities for me to progress in my career?

While sounding overambitious and presumptuous isn't a good thing, asking this question will be a good demonstration of your ambition and a willingness to be around to help the company grow for a long period of time.

8. How do you see this company in few years?

This goes to show that you have an interest in the growth and goals of the company. It also shows commitment and provides information to your interviewers on your values and how your goals are in line with those of the organization.

9. What is your definition of success?

Having a rough idea of what the company you are applying to values and the way and manner they provide feedback can give you an idea of the culture and traditions of the company you are about to join. Additionally, you can have some basic knowledge of your prospective boss and his ideas.

10. What's the next step?

Asking this question helps you know the next thing in your job search process and when the company will likely contact you. Asking this question is a good way of showing confidence and a burning desire for the job.

11. Who do you think would be the ideal candidate for this position, and how do I compare?

This is not only meant to give you an idea of whether you will be hired or not, but it can be of great use to you in preparing for other job searches and interviews in the future. However, you have to be able to keep your cool here in case the interviewer says something you do not like when it comes to comparing your performance to their ideal candidate.

12. Who would I be reporting to? Are those three people on the same team or different teams? What's the pecking order?

This question is meant to give you more knowledge of the job you are being interviewed for. It will help you understand the organizational structure of the team. If the proper description is given to you by the interviewer, you will have full knowledge of the people you are going to work with if you are hired.

13. Who do you consider as your major competitors? How are you better?

Even before asking this, you must have a general idea of the major competitors of the company. Here, you are likely going to know more about the selling points of the company which the interviewer will highlight as things that made them better than their competitors.

14. Do you have any hesitations about my qualifications?

Think about this question as an honest assessment of your

qualifications by the interviewer. Accept any hesitations mentioned without showing signs of discontentment.

15. Can you give me an example of how I would collaborate with my manager?

Although this may look like you're being overly ambitious, it shows your readiness to work with your manager. This question gives you the opportunity to take note of a few of the things that are required of you, if employed.

16. Can you tell me what steps need to be completed before your company can generate an offer?

An insight to this question will help you know if there are other things you need to do before you are finally hired. It is important to take note of the answers as you may have to refer to them later.

17. What have past employees done to succeed in this position?

This is an important question that may be pivotal to your success in the position you are vying for. Asking this question also reveals your readiness to optimize your performance for the benefit of the company.

18. How do you help your team grow professionally?

Consider this as a way of knowing whether the company will be of benefit to your career or not. If there is no clear answer, it could be an indication that there is no help offered by the company to its team.

19. When your staff comes to you with conflicts, how do you respond?

Since conflict resolution is one of the important parts of how a company manages its staff, knowing how those at the helm of affairs respond to conflicts is essential.

20. Will I have an opportunity to meet those who would be part of my staff/my manager during the interview process?

While this may sound unnecessary, the answer may help you prepare for the discreet evaluation of your potential co-workers.

21. I read X about your CEO in Y magazine. Can you tell me more about this?

Without a doubt, this question reveals that you have been following the progress of the company for a while. It is even capable of increasing your odds of getting the job.

22. What's your staff turnover rate and what are you doing to reduce it?

This question can help you make a decision about whether the job is worth it or not. It might also give you an idea of the level of satisfaction employees derive from working at the company.

23. Is there anyone else I need to meet with? Is there anyone else you would like me to meet with?

Whether a superior or colleague, there may be someone

else you need to meet before getting the job, so don't hesitate to ask this question. If possible, ask about the relevance of the person to your chance of being hired.

24. How would you score the company on living up to its core values? What's the one thing you're working to improve on?

Every company has core values; hence, you should ask about the efforts of the company towards achieving these values and improving them.

25. Beyond the hard skills required to successfully perform this job, what soft skills would serve the company and position best?

Knowing the soft skills that suit the company and position can help you improve yourself to perform more effectively.

If you follow the seven steps in this chapter, your odds of turning your next interview into a job offer will increase significantly. Keep in mind, however, that if by some chance you don't get the job, there's another useful step you can take: Phone the company and politely ask why you didn't get hired. Hiring managers are often surprisingly willing to tell you which skill they felt you were lacking (so long as you're respectful) allowing you to use unsuccessful interviews as a form of career guidance. Experience is, after all, the best teacher: Learn from it, combine it with the correct techniques, and keep practicing until you master the interview process. While it's a lot of hard work, the job you get will ultimately be more than worth it.

CHAPTER 13

How To Follow Up After A Job Interview

A lot of job seekers often seem hesitant to follow up after an interview. It is natural to feel that you may be bugging the interviewers and to wonder whether a telephone call will hinder or help your chances of getting a second interview or even the job.

A lot of human resource managers these days accept phone calls as their preferred means of communication from candidates. Below is how hiring managers like to be contacted (Menlo, 2012):

- Email --- 87%
- Phone call --- 81%
- Handwritten note --- 38%
- Social media --- 27%
- Text message --- 10%

The first three of the options are the best. Human resource managers and interviewers prefer a handwritten or emailed thank you note or a telephone call. Texting doesn't appeal at all to most human resource managers – they will look upon you as a casual person who is not serious. You are also advised not send messages through social media since recruiters or potential bosses are not your friends on most social networks. Sending a message through LinkedIn is in line too if you are already communicating on there. You need to be as professional as you were during the interview no matter the form your follow-up takes. The few things talked about will help you be at your best when following up on job interviews.

1. *Never send out a generic thank you email:* sending a thank you email after an interview can be the key to landing the job. You can send a handwritten thank note but in whatever you do, never send a generic thank you email. If there is no sense of urgency, you may still want to send a quick thank you email together with a traditional note or letter. In this way, you will be resounding your interest in the offer sooner than later. Now in addition to thanking the hiring managers in the email, you can use it to address issues and concerns that came up during the interview.

You can send a thank you email as an interview follow-up, use it to restate why you are the best candidate for the job. Also, remind them about your qualifications and how you can make significant contributions to the growth of the organization.

The thank you letter can be an ideal opportunity to talk about anything of importance that your interviewer overlooked or that you neglected to answer thoroughly. In addition to your thank you note not being generic; it should also be brief and straight to the point.

2. *Always show the benefit you will bring to the company:*
every business is operating to make profits. They wouldn't just
hire anyone for the sake of it. That explains why you really
need to sell yourself to the interviewers during and after the
interview through thank you notes. Again, just like during
the normal interview, reiterate why you are the best fit for the
role and the values you will be bringing to the organization
to help them attain their goals. The keyword here is to sell
yourself once more.

3. *A few strong reasons or key points why the organization
needs you:* Your thank you note should have three to four
strong points of why the company needs your skills and experience. It is quite important. Again, don't be generic in writing
these points, instead tailor them to what transpired during
the interview. Luckily in the interview, you asked them what
they are looking for in the perfect candidate, or the qualities
they believe a candidate will possess to excel in the position.
Use that hint to come up with your strong points of what
you will be bringing to the organization, if hired. Point out
all the qualities you have that they also said they are looking
for so that you will stand out. You can take it a step further
by giving an example of how you've demonstrated these skills
maybe in a project you carried out while in college.

Lastly, do not forget to answer the question "what problem
will hiring you solve." This is very important as no organization
is willing to hire a redundant staff. They want someone who
will come into their team and address one of their numerous
problems and challenges.

The above only pertains to sending written thank you notes. If you are going to call in to say thank you after an interview, you have to call your interviewer directly. Calling within 24 hours of the interview is ideal. Don't leave a message if you get a voicemail on your first attempt. Rather, try again to see if you can catch the interviewer in an available moment by the phone. Early or late in the day are the best times to call since people are less likely to be in interviews or engagements by then. If you are, however, unable to reach your interviewer after so many attempts, leave a message with the following information:

- Your name
- The job title you interviewed for
- When you interviewed
- A thank you
- Request for the person to call you back if he needs additional information
- Your phone number

Here is a sample message you can drop: Hi Mr. Bass! This is Jane Solano calling. I interviewed yesterday for the position of an android developer and wanted to thank you for taking your time to with meet me. I enjoyed our conversation. If there's any additional information I can provide, please do not hesitate to get in touch. You can reach me on 222-222-2222. Thanks again, and I hope to hear from you soon.

If you reach the interviewer you are lucky — a lot of people screen all their calls these days. Be brief and to the point, thank the hiring manager for their time, recap your qualifications, then ask if there is any additional information the interviewer would like to know or if there is any further information you can provide on your background or experience.

If there was anything you didn't mention in the interview that you now wish you had mentioned but didn't, take this opportunity to share it with the interviewer.

Tips for Writing a Strong Thank You Email

1. *Send an email to each interviewer:* If you were interviewed by many people, send individual messages to every person you interviewed with. You have to modify your message so that each interviewer receives a thank you message that is unique. It will help if you have the contact information for each thank you email.

2. *Use a professional subject line:* Provide just enough information about why you are sending the message in the subject line. Include the phrase "Thank you" and either the title of the job you interviewed for or your name. You can choose to add both.

Reference

Menlo, P. (2012, June 14). Survey Reveals Email, Phone Call Are Preferred Methods for Post-Interview Follow-Up. Accountemps. Retrieved from http://accountemps.rhi.mediaroom.com/thank-you.

CHAPTER 14

How To Negotiate A Salary–Get What You Deserve

Salary negotiation is usually a critical part of the job search process. It can be the difference between a frustrating career and a fulfilling one. You can be haunted for years by a poorly negotiated salary, hence the importance of mastering the basics of negotiating salaries before you find yourself in a heated salary dialogue with an employer.

Salary negotiations are important for both the potential employee and the employer because if not anchored well, the outcome becomes an employee who is disgruntled or an overpaid employee who, in the estimation of the employer, doesn't deserve what he earns. Such an employee would hence be considered unqualified for any form of increase in compensation over some period of time.

Below are ten tips to put you in a better position to negotiate the salary you deserve.

1. Anticipate hard questions.

You should expect tough questions during a salary negotiation. In as much as the organization might value your skills, qualifications, and experiences, your potential employer will strive to offer you a lower salary than you deserve. This is why it is called a negotiation.

In the past, hard questions used to knock candidates off balance but not anymore. Anticipating them will help you get prepared for the eventuality. Such questions might include:

- Why should we hire you?
- Do you currently have another offer you're considering?
- If we offered you a job tomorrow, would you accept?

Whatever the question, try not to tell a lie or give a nervous response. The responses you give might turn around to haunt you as they both tend to have the same effect.

When asked tough questions, answer them directly rather than attempting to be evasive. For instance, when giving an answer to the first question, you are to show why you are the most qualified candidate for the position.

When asked an unanticipated hard question, another thing that might happen is that you would likely find yourself suddenly making attempts to say something pleasing and nice to the ears of your prospective employer and stand the risk of losing value in the eyes of the individual on the other side of the table. Worse still, it is largely unattractive.

2. Understand the difference between gross salary and net salary.

Your gross salary refers to the total package that you are entitled to before tax and other statutory deductions, while your net salary is the specific amount of money you go home with after deductions from your gross salary.

To put things in layman terms, your gross salary will always be higher than your net salary. For example, your gross salary might be $90,000, while your net salary would be $82,000 per annum.

Therefore, when asked for your salary from your former employer, make sure you clarify. If asked, you could say, "My net salary was $82,000 from XYZ Company." By saying this, your potential employer knows that your gross salary would be much higher, which puts you in a better position to negotiate.

3. Request for offer review.

Request for offer review is normally used during salary negotiation by the prospective employee to aim for the highest salary possible. You should have a counter offer ready before getting to the stage of salary negotiation.

However, remember that the same way a counter offer works in your favor, it also works for the employer who will most likely use it to keep your salary within the current market range.

So, this is how it works: during negotiation, the employer has a tendency to drop a figure on the table saying something like: "We're offering you $80,000 for the position of..." and might quickly add some other benefits you would enjoy. This is the time to unveil your counter offer to this first job offer from your potential employer.

Again, your counter offer may not be expressly approved by most employers. Rather, they will come up with their slightly revised offer to counter yours.

In some cases, however, the employer will accept your counter offer and give you an employment offer or leave you with the famous line: "We will get back to you in the shortest possible time. It was a pleasure talking with you."

As mentioned earlier, salary negotiation is not just about the salary. While presenting your counter offer, use the opportunity to negotiate for other things such as number of working hours, benefit packages, pension plan and severance packages, etc.

4. Strengthen your negotiation with research.

You have to do a lot of research for a salary negotiation. Research the salaries for your position and industry by visiting websites such as Salary.com, Payscale.com, and Glassdoor. com to successfully negotiate your salary. This research will give you the needed edge to negotiate fairly. You don't want to appear weak during a negotiation. It can leave you losing out on an opportunity to earn more.

In clear terms, do not underestimate or neglect the essence of research. Negotiation without facts will most likely be unsuccessful. You don't want that, do you? Before the negotiation stage, you should make inquiries of what others with such roles in other organizations earn. This gives you an idea of how you should react to any offer from your potential employer. It also helps you decide what offer from your potential employee to consider 'reasonable,' 'way below industry standard' or 'really impressive.' Remember that you must have compelling facts.

You can consider reaching out to your mentors or other rightly placed people to get your facts.

Most importantly, you should try to find out what the organization pays employees for the role in question. This is where research comes in. Do your research on what the salary range is. With this information, you will find yourself in a more comfortable position to negotiate.

5. Don't constitute a nuisance.

During a salary negotiation, it is better to avoid expressions, utterances, and body language that reduce your likeability. This is because the less likable you appear to be, the lower your chances of getting what you're negotiating from your potential employer.

What we are talking about here goes beyond being polite. Rather, it emphasizes staying calm enough to ask for more without sounding greedy. You can achieve this by throwing some light on shortfalls in the offer of the employer without sounding petty. One way to do this is to practice (getting interviewed) with a friend until you are used to it.

If your potential employer likes the level of confidence you show or the way you negotiate, it puts you in a better position to receive an improved offer.

6. Re-emphasize your availability and interest.

The moment your potential employer starts suspecting that you are not available to be hired, they will naturally soft pedal in their quest to hire you. This is because you have shown to them that they cannot get you whether the offer is improved or not. Chasing shadows isn't something anyone enjoys and that's exactly what your prospective employer would notice if you do not make it clear that you are available to be hired.

Therefore, if you are seriously in need of the job, make it seem glaring and convey the message using a few words about how much you are aligned with the goals of the company and would be willing to join them provided you're given the right offer. If you have an offer from another company, now would be a good time to say it and make it clear that if you had the chance to pick, you would pick them (prospective employer) over other offers you currently have.

Hit the nail on the head by reaffirming the fact that you are ready to leave all other offers and spell out the specific conditions under which you would gladly accept their offer.

7. Approach it as a business deal.

You should never take salary negotiations for granted for any reason because it will determine how much you will earn for your effort as an employee within an organization.

Therefore, you should have a plan the same way you would have for a business transaction. You don't want to accept whatever is presented to you especially when you know how much you are worth. Now is the chance you have to sell yourself to your potential employer because the moment you accept the job, objecting to the offer might raise your employer's eyebrows about your decision making prowess.

8. Practice as much as you can.

Shy people are afraid of confrontations same as most other people. For some people, the thought of even attending the interview and sitting opposite an interviewer makes them feel uneasy.

The best way to get out of this is to practice. Yes! You can stand in front of a mirror and ask yourself questions regarding salary negotiation. Better still, get a friend to play the part of the potential employer and ask you questions. Additionally, practice reactions to different scenarios, especially rejection. The scenarios should include those where the prospective employer agrees to accept your salary bid as well as those where there is an outright rejection of your counter offer.

9. Know who you are negotiating with.

It is of utmost importance that you know the precise person who is negotiating with you during salary negotiations. Is it the CEO of the company that is interviewing you or the HR representative? Knowing this is important for many reasons. One such reason is that while you can afford to throw a flurry of questions about the offer at an HR representative, you wouldn't want to risk annoying your boss with such at this point of the recruitment process. Organizations do not do salary negotiations. People conduct them. To be able to influence the decision of whoever you are negotiating with, there must be some level of understanding of who this person is.

10. Bring something impressive to the table.

Before you get to the point of actual negotiation, let your potential employer know what your capabilities are and cite real examples of this with a project you have done. Sell your talents, skills and problem-solving abilities to the hiring manager to show the value you bring to the position. Give specific work related examples that will help in salary negotiations.

The tips discussed above put into perspective the value of negotiating for a salary offer from your potential employer. Be reminded that the more you put these tips into practice, the better for you and your career.

CHAPTER 15

Dress For Success–Image Is Everything!

How you dress for a job interview is very important and crucial as the first impression you leave the interviewer with will have a substantial impact on how the interview will progress thereby adding to your overall performance.

Knowing how to dress for a job interview is an age-old conundrum. Fashions come and go, but style is something that remains constant, and, for both formal and informal interviews, there are a few hard and fast rules. There's no room for experimentation in your interview wardrobe, so you must look your best as image is everything.

Here we will discuss the best ways men and women should properly dress for an interview to increase their chances of landing that dream job.

The Formal Interview

Your aspiration should be to dress one notch above what you would typically consider suitable for work. And that, of course, means the job that you're interviewing for. You could decide to get a clear indication of what people are wearing by hanging around the employee parking lot at clocking off time, but as a general rule of thumb, a suit is going to be the best wear for both men and women.

Suits never go out of fashion. There's always someone out there sporting a two (or three) piece suit. A particular recent trend appears to be, what I like to call the shiny suit. These suits are made of a cloth that looks like it could produce its own light with the sun, while it's perfectly acceptable for a nightclub or a wedding, it should not be attempted for a job interview – unless that interview happens to be for a boy band.

Women

You have the choice of trousers or skirt. The rule with a skirt is that the hemline should be no more than a sixth of an inch above the knee. Black is always a go-to color. Brown, navy, and, in the summer, a lighter plain color are also excellent colors for women.

Patterns should be avoided. Add a touch of color with a scarf, but the shoes should be moderate. If you must wear heels, let the height be moderate. Shoes can be the female equivalent of the shiny suit. Going for a plain blouse or one with a simple stripe is the perfect option.

Men

Dark, sober colors are always good, and cotton should be preferred over linen, even in the summer – linen creases quite easily. Shoes should be black or brown – brown with a brown or blue suit, black with a black, grey or blue suit. You should not try mixing brown and black and always go for leather instead of suede.

In like manner, avoid garish patterns on ties that can distract an interviewer. The tie is supposed to complement the whole ensemble, so it should be matched with the suit as well as the shirt. It's always easiest to go with a plain, white shirt and a non-patterned, single-colored tie. Not one that features Homer Simpson or Captain America. The same goes for your socks, and yes, the interviewer will notice.

Business Casual

Some organizations like to test your ability to interpret fashion etiquette by setting a business casual dress code. For both genders, casual trousers and blazers can be blended and matched, ties dispensed with and even shoes can be less formal. But if it seems confusing, just follow these rules:

No jeans, no trainers, and no T-shirts. Because it is business casual.

In the final analysis, if you look great, you'll feel great, and if you feel great, there will be a much greater chance of you acing your interview. Whatever you decide to wear, I would recommend that you start with a fairly safe, uncomplicated canvas and add a splash, but no more, of your personality with a well-chosen accessory.

If you get the chance to try on your outfit a couple of days in advance, you will be able to get any dry cleaning done and come up with a contingency should something either not fit, or have a rip or hole in it.

One final note: make sure your shoes are polished.

Six things you should never wear to an interview

1. Ill-fitting clothes

It is better to wear an outfit that is tailored to suit you rather than anything that looks or feels too tight or too short. Wearing short skirts and dresses that are hard to sit in will give a wrong impression of you.

2. Jeans

Staying away from jeans at an interview is smart even if you will wear them as part of your work attire. They are not professional at all, although they can be casual and comfortable.

3. Colors

Don't wear bright colors. Stick with the basic: a black, brown or blue suit.

4. Loud makeup

Tone down your makeup; keep it simple and natural.

5. Obvious bras

This goes to the women. Always wear a nude bra under business attire because they rarely ever show.

6. Hats

Hats either distract the interviewer or prevent the two of you from making eye contact.

CHAPTER 16

How To Create An Effective 30-60-90 Day Employment Action Plan (Hiring Managers Will Love This)

How to Create a Successful 30-60-90 Day Employment Action Plan That Will Impress Hiring Managers and Secure Employment

The first three months of a new job are "time critical" where performance is concerned: These 90 days form a probation period wherein your hiring manager will constantly be evaluating your capabilities. During this period, you will be adjusting to a whole new environment with new people, a different schedule, and the emotional burden of stress and anxiety. In short, it's incredibly easy to become disorganized during the first 90 days of a new job—and of course, this creates a state of confusion which often leads to errors being made. As the old saying goes, "Those who fail to plan, plan to fail."

This is why you need what is known as a "30-60-90 day Action Plan." A 30-60-90 Day Action Plan sets forth what you hope to accomplish during the first month of your new job, the second month, and the third month; it ensures goals are clear and suggests solutions to possible problems before they have a chance to crop up. In addition to making the first three months of your job easier to handle, having an Action Plan is an excellent way to impress your hiring manager. This is because he or she will see that you're serious about excelling at your new job and will appreciate the work you have done (and the research you have conducted). Resultantly, your hiring manager will be able to sitdown with you and discuss potential issues and solutions before you're actively working. Additionally, you will come across as an excellent hire because you will convey to your employer that you are more than someone who simply shows up and does their work; you're an employee with a vision, someone who will go the extra mile to grow with the company and proactively shape its future.

The 30-60-90 Day Action Plan: Getting Started

Ideally, you should be prepared to revise your Action Plan at several key intervals: You should create the first copy of your Action Plan before your first interview, revise it during the later stages of the interview process, and refine it once again after your first week on the job. This will show your employer that you have an excellent aptitude for integrating new information into existing strategies, as well as making the plan more relevant.

Before writing your Action Plan, it's essential to do lots of research into the company you are applying to. The more specific you can make your plan, the better. Look into practical details such as any software the company is using to perform key functions, the name of the training program they put new employees through, etc. You should also investigate the current affairs of the business. To find this information, take the following steps:

- *Visit the company's website.* The company website should give you an overview of the company's products, services, mission statement, etc., allowing you to begin discovering how those products are created or how those services are performed (assuming there are areas you are not already familiar with). You will also get a sense of how big the company is and how they conduct business; this should give you some context to gauge their expectations.

- *Check Google for news about the company.* A Google news search can reveal whether or not the company is growing, what problems the company may be having or developments the company is going through, and how the general public views the company. Once you understand the challenges the company is facing, you can write your Action Plan in such a way that you appear ready and able to help the company overcome its hurdles and continue to grow.

- *Visit LinkedIn.* A company's corporate page on LinkedIn will often provide you with the information you can't get by just reading the company's website; additionally, you will be able to locate the profiles of executives and other employees who work at the company. Assess what their skills are, what their background of experience is like, and how long they have worked for the company.

• *Check out the company's Facebook and Twitter pages.* While Facebook and Twitter might not be quite as informative as LinkedIn, their more casual atmosphere means that employees often express more of who they are on these social media services. You can, therefore, glean valuable information about corporate culture and communication styles by browsing Twitter and LinkedIn.

• *Talk to your recruiter.* Your recruiter may have additional insider information not covered online, so it's usually worthwhile to discuss the company you're applying to with them.

Finally, remember that while you find many guides and even templates for Action Plans online, you shouldn't be afraid to think creatively and draft something uniquely your own (just try to keep it between one and four pages in length). As is the case when writing a resume or cover letter, if you're unsure of how to write an effective Action Plan, it's a good idea to seek help from an experienced mentor.

How to Write a 30-60-90 Day Action Plan

While no one can tell you exactly what to put in your 30-60-90 Day Action Plan as goals and objectives vary widely from job to job, some general themes tend to apply across industries. Below you will find a sample outline of a 30-60-90 Day Action Plan, complete with possible goals you can alter to fit your customized Action Plan:

Introduction

Your 30-60-90 Day Action Plan should start with an introduction section describing an overview of what you would like to accomplish during your initial three months on the job. Keep this section upbeat, engaging, and brief to reduce the overall length of your Action Plan.

Section One: The First 30 Days

This is the initial "learning stage" of your new job, so you should keep the goals you outline in this section attainable and realistic. During the first 30 days of your new job, you can expect to engage in employee training, be introduced to other team members, and learn about the organization's products and services. You will also come to understand its systems and procedures. As such, your objectives during the first 30 days should reflect a desire to learn more about the company, its business strategy, people you are working with, and so on.

Sample objectives for this section include:

- Understand how the company's mission statement and unique vision is brought to life. Investigate the plans and practices that help the company abide by its core values while still delivering a quality product in a timely fashion.

- Establish a solid working relationship with your boss. Find out what they expect of you and sketch out a plan for how you can deliver on those expectations reliably and accurately.

- Begin forming productive professional relationships

with your new coworkers. Assess team dynamics and communication style, understand how the team would like you to begin working on tasks or projects at hand, and form professional connections with the team on social media.

- Learn about the company's customers and clients. Research the demographics of the company's customers (their average age level, interests, and so on); investigate how to communicate effectively with customers and clients based on this information and the existing knowledge of coworkers. Familiarize yourself with the expectations of customers and clients.

- Start to integrate yourself into the existing company culture. By getting to know your coworkers and connecting with them on social media, you will be able to gain a sense of what the overall company culture is like. Additionally, you should be sure to attend any company events during this time.

Section Two: The First 60 Days

Once you have spent some time observing the company's procedures and employees and learning the ropes of your new position, you will be able to segue into proactively adding value to the organization. Between the 30 and 60 day mark, you should have your eyes on mastering the "best practices" of the organization (and your industry as a whole), setting goals, gathering feedback from your boss or supervisor, building working relationships with your team members, and assessing the relative efficiency of company processes and procedures (don't forget to also look outside your department when doing so).

Suggested goals for the second 30 days include:

- Fully integrate your skills into the dynamics of the team. Showcase what you do well and look for areas where your skills can help the team be more successful and efficient. While the first 30 days of a new job are mostly about listening rather than talking, during the first 60 days, you should begin wading into team discussions more frequently and making useful contributions.

- Brainstorm ways in which your unique skills and vision can accelerate company growth. After working 30 days at your new job, you should know enough about the company's growth strategy to start generating ideas for how your skills and experience can speed up that growth. If you're unsure about the company's growth strategy, feel free to discuss it with your boss (or another approachable senior figure within the company); this will show initiative and yield useful information.

- Take on new and interesting tasks without feeling limited to your known set of responsibilities. The first 30 days of a new job are usually spent learning basic duties, but by the time you start counting the second 30 days, you should be able to branch out a bit and take on new tasks which fall outside of your predetermined responsibilities. Just make sure to get the input of your boss and your team before taking on auxiliary tasks.

- Review your boss's expectations of you. You should verify that the plan you came up with in your first 30 days of working (for meeting your boss's expectations) is adequate; ask your boss for suggestions regarding anything you could be doing better.

Section 3: The Full 90 Days

As you near the 90 day mark, you should be finding your feet as a permanent employee; this section covers the "transitional period" that will move you away from being a trainee and help you gain a solid understanding of your role within the company and how to carry it out with the utmost efficiency and accuracy. As your confidence and knowledge grow, you should look for opportunities to demonstrate your leadership capabilities. Goals for this section can include:

- Take a proactive role in company events. You should be familiar enough with company procedures and processes by this point to be ready to tackle new challenges without your boss or colleagues guiding you. While it is, of course, still essential to seek the input of other team members, you should have the ability to work independently as needed and think up viable, innovative strategies on your own.
- Become a planner and a strategist. Pay attention to what is going on in the company so that you remain

abreast of upcoming projects; start thinking of problems and solutions before new projects are underway. Take an active role in the project planning process and make sure to keep revising your strategies to enhance company growth as you learn more and as new challenges arise.

- Expand your network. By this stage, you should have an established working relationship with your team—but you shouldn't stop there. Actively work at expanding your network; talk to people in other departments, make an effort to get to know the company's clients and partners, and make connections via social media with others in your industry.

- Look for opportunities to get more involved in your company and industry. Now that you have mastered the basics of performing your new duties, you should have enough time to get out there and broaden your horizons. Look for clubs you can join, industry events you can attend, and company boards or committees you can apply to. This will both connect you with a steady stream of new knowledge and enhance your level of influence within the company and your industry.

- Review your growth as an employee. Take stock of everything you have learned since starting your new job and don't be afraid to reward yourself for your progress—you've earned it! By this stage you and your boss should have reached a point of clarity where expectations are concerned, so you can focus on continuing your learning and wait for your next performance review to revisit these expectations.

- Refine company processes and procedures as necessary. With input from your boss, work on improving the company's strategies and practices wherever you feel it's necessary. Keep a sharp eye on existing processes and procedures and work to identify inefficiencies.

- Strengthen your team. By now you should understand your team's dynamics and communication styles. If you see any places where communication is breaking down, and team members are not getting the best from one another, feel free to step in and offer helpful mediation. If you see another team member struggling with a task, or there is now a newer member on the team than yourself, feel free to step into the role of mentor.

- Gain a more in-depth understanding of client negotiations. As you become more and more familiar with the company's clients, you can take a more active role in negotiating parameters with them. At this point you are no longer becoming part of the organization—you are one of its many representatives and should take initiative accordingly.

The Bottom Line

While the details of your 30-60-90 Day Action Plan should be adapted to fit your unique position and the needs of your industry, the overarching theme should be as follows: Your plan should lay out a realistic and logical path that will take you from being the company's newest employee to one of its freshest, innovative, and effective leaders. Remember, when a company hires a new employee, they are looking for more than just a certain set of skills and the right background of experience: They deeply desire to inject new life into the organization, to shake up its existing systems and find better ways of doing things. By organizing and prioritizing your tasks on a 30-60-90-day basis, you free up your problem-solving abilities so that you can use them to challenge the status quo as soon as you have safely learned the ropes of your new position. And, most importantly, you show your hiring manager from the outset exactly what kind of value you plan to add to the organization.

Conclusion

Finding that dream job can often be time-consuming and takes lots of commitment. Locating a position that matches your needs, interests, abilities, and goals may not be easy, but it is time well spent as you go about launching your career. The process need not be frustrating. In fact, if you follow the strategies outlined in this book, your job search will be one of the most rewarding experiences of your life. However, if you haven't been achieving the best results in your job search, take some time to consider these points:

- Thousands of positions become available and are filled every month even in the toughest economic times.
- The job doesn't usually go to the most qualified candidate but to the candidates who know the most about how to stand out and land the job.
- Your academic qualification does not mandate the type of job you will get. But by presenting your abilities and skills properly, you can benefit from a wide range of opportunities.
- Your initial decision is not necessarily where you will spend your entire career. The average graduate this year will have seven or eight positions in his/her lifetime in at least four or more different career fields. Nonetheless, the first job you get may have an impact on the types of jobs you will be able to successfully compete

for in the future.

- The more focused you are in your search, the more you can concentrate on the opportunities in the field of your choice, and the more efficient you will be in your job-search strategies. In conducting a job search, lack of focus is not a virtue but demanding the best of yourself is.

You can ask yourself this: "How much do I want this job?" Take ten minutes, dig deep and think about what you deserve.

Write down the things you think you deserve. And in doing so, don't aim low for yourself, cross out every negative thought and write a great dream for yourself! Write some details around the awesome dreams you've thought for yourself. Stare at it. Let it soak in.

With fearlessness, embrace what you deserve and demand the best from your choices of thought and action today. What will come to you will be more of what you want. You'll see it when you believe it. But no matter how small your efforts are, you've got to wake up and get things done tomorrow anyway. So you might as well wake up deserving an awesome day, and then command that it is one. Then go to sleep. Repeat until you get the job you desire.

You deserve the best!

Get hired for the job you want!

To your success,

Robert Moment

The Get Hired Expert

P.S. You've got what it takes to succeed. Believe in yourself and succeed in life.

About The Author

Robert Moment is The Get Hired Expert and Job Interview Coach who helps ambitious recent college graduates get hired for jobs and make more money.

Visit www.GettingaJobAfterCollege.com to learn more about Job Search Strategies and Interview Preparation That Will Get You Hired.

Contact Robert Moment for Speaking, Seminar and Inter-view Coaching Opportunities at Robert@GettingaJobAfter-College.com